Ilex Foundation Series 13

FERDOWSI'S *SHĀHNĀMA*: MILLENNIAL PERSPECTIVES

Also in the Ilex Foundation Series

Dreaming across Boundaries: The Interpretation of Dreams in Islamic Lands
edited by Louise Marlow

Strī: Women in Epic Mahābhārata
by Kevin McGRATH

Persian Literature and Judeo-Persian Culture: Collected Writings of Sorour S. Soroudi
edited by Houchang Chehabi

The Rhetoric of Biography: Narrating Lives in Persianate Societies
edited by L. Marlow

Jaya: Performance in Epic Mahābhārata
by Kevin McGRATH

The History *of Beyhaqi (The History of Sultan Masʿud of Ghazna, 1030–1041) by Abu'l-Fażl Beyhaqi*
translated and with commentaries by Clifford Edmund Bosworth
fully revised and with further commentary by Mohsen Ashtiany

The Last of the Rephaim: Conquest and Cataclysm in the Heroic Ages of Ancient Israel
by Brian R. Doak

Ruse and Wit: Humorous Writing in Arabic, Turkish, and Persian Narrative
edited by Dominic Parvis Brookshaw

Kṛṣṇa: Friendship in Epic Mahābhārata
by Kevin McGRATH

On the Wonders of Land and Sea: Persianate Travel Writing
edited by Roberta Micallef and Sunil Sharma

Poet and Hero in the Persian Book of Kings
third edition
by Olga M. Davidson

Comparative Literature and Classical Persian Poetics
second edition
by Olga M. Davidson

FERDOWSI'S *SHĀHNĀMA*

MILLENNIAL PERSPECTIVES

Edited by
Olga M. Davidson
and
Marianna Shreve Simpson

Ilex Foundation
Boston, Massachusetts

Center for Hellenic Studies
Trustees for Harvard University
Washington, D. C.

K. R. Cama Oriental Institute
Mumbai, India

Distributed by Harvard University Press
Cambridge, Massachusetts, and London, England

Ferdowsi's *Shāhnāma*: Millennial Perspectives
Edited by Olga M. Davidson and Marianna Shreve Simpson

Published by Ilex Foundation, Boston, Massachusetts; the Center for Hellenic Studies, Trustees for Harvard University, Washington, D.C.; and the K. R. Cama Oriental Institute, Mumbai

Distributed by Harvard University Press, Cambridge, Massachusetts and London, England

Production editor: Christopher Dadian
Cover design: Joni Godlove
Printed in the United States of America

Cover images are adapted from: Fragmentary Star Tile, early 13th century, ceramic over-glaze painted with enamel and luster. Courtesy Museum of Fine Arts Boston, 31.495. Photograph © 2013 Museum of Fine Arts.

Library of Congress Cataloging-in-Publication Data

Ferdowsi's Shahnama : millennial perspectives / edited by Olga M. Davidson and Marianna Shreve Simpson.
pages cm. -- (Ilex Foundation series ; 13)
Includes bibliographical references and index.
ISBN 978-0-674-72680-2 (alk. paper)
1. Firdawsi. Shahnamah. I. Davidson, Olga M. editor of compilation. II. Simpson, Marianna Shreve, 1949- editor of compilation.
PK6459.F48 2013
891'.5511--dc23

2013030802

CONTENTS

Preface vii

Olga M. Davidson
Interweavings of Book and Performance in the Making of the *Shāhnāma* of Ferdowsi: Extrapolations from the Narrative of the So-Called Bāysonghori Preface 1

Anna Krasnowolska
Ferdowsi's *Dāstān*—An Autonomous Narrative Unit? 12

Firuza Abdullaeva
The Legend of Siyāvosh or the Legend of Yusof? 28

Charles Melville
The Story of Furūd in the *Shāhnāma* and Elsewhere and the Apportionment of Blame 58

Marianna Shreve Simpson
Shāhnāma Images and *Shāhnāma* Settings in Medieval Iran 72

Sunil Sharma
The Production of Mughal *Shāhnāmas*: Imperial, Sub-Imperial, and Provincial Manuscripts 86

Index 109

PREFACE

The millennium of the *Shāhnāma,* Iran's epic Book of Kings, completed by the poet Abu'l Qāsim Ferdowsi in 1010 CE, was celebrated beginning in 2010 by a multitude of publications, conferences, exhibitions, and other events worldwide.[1] Among the various scholarly gatherings was a "Seminar on *The Shahnameh*" held at the K. R. Cama Oriental Institute in Mumbai on 8–9 January 2011. Founded in 1916, the Cama Oriental Institute enjoys a widespread reputation for its significant role in promoting and advancing scholarship on Oriental religion, history, and culture, with particular emphasis on Zoroastrianism and Iranian studies, through its extensive library holdings, annual *Journal* and other publications, research projects, lectures, courses, fellowships, and essay competitions. In 2001 it initiated a series of National Seminars on diverse topics, starting with "Ferdowsi and His *Shahnameh*," and two years later published the proceedings of this inaugural meeting.[2]

The January 2011 "Seminar on *The Shahnameh*" was thus the Cama Institute's second contribution within a decade—and more specifically within the first decade of the twenty-first century—to showcase research on Ferdowsi's literary masterpiece one thousand years on. Organized by Muncherji N. M. Cama, president of the K. R. Cama Oriental Institute, and by Dr. Mrs. Nawaz B. Mody, its joint honorary secretary, and generously supported by the government of India's Ministry of Culture, the "Seminar on *The Shahnameh*" addressed six themes pertinent to current scholarly engagement with this venerable epic poem. These included the *Shāhnāma*'s pre-Islamic origins; questions of orality and textuality; the poem's literary and textual heritage in Persianate societies; its reception in later Persian, Byzantine, and Armenian epics; the rich artistic tradition inspired by the stories and characters in Ferdowsi's poem; and the collection and codicology of *Shāhnāma* manuscripts. The complete program, with the roster of speakers and abstracts of their presentations, appears in a handsome booklet distributed on the occasion of the seminar's festive inauguration.

1. A listing of millennial events appears at the end of the entry for "Šāh-nāma iv. Illustrations," *Encyclopaedia Iranica* on-line (accessed 22 July 2013).

2. *Proceedings of the All India Seminar on Ferdowsi and his* Shahnameh, *held on 9th–11th November 2001* (Mumbai: Culture House of the Islamic Republic of Iran and K. R. Cama Oriental Institute, 2003).

Like the K. R. Cama Oriental Institute, the Ilex Foundation sponsors scholarly research and publications in the humanities, with particular emphasis on the civilizations of the Near East and Mediterranean from the second millennium BCE to the present.[3] Fostering greater public appreciation of the history and cultural traditions of Iran, including Persian literature and art, has been central to the Foundation's mission and activities since its inception in Boston, Massachusetts in 1999. Indeed, the Foundation heralded this milestone with a First Ferdowsi Conference held at Harvard University that same year.

The Ilex Foundation team was delighted, therefore, when the Cama Institute agreed to a proposal to cooperate in publishing selected papers from the 2011 *Shāhnāma* seminar held in Mumbai. The resulting volume, part of a publication series produced in partnership with Harvard's Center for Hellenic Studies, speaks to the deep humanistic concerns shared by institutions in the United States and India alike, and to the scholarly benefits and mutual understanding to be gained from such international collaboration. This co-sponsored publication is yet another testament to the enduring appeal and impact of the verses and values of Ferdowsi's *Shāhnāma.*

The six papers compiled here from among the full complement of those presented in Mumbai draw together various of the seminar's principle themes, particularly concerning the *Shāhnāma*'s narrative structure, the source and meaning of specific *Shāhnāma* stories and their appearance in other literary texts, and the poem's visual history and artistic transmission both within and beyond Iran. Given that the Cama Institute originally invited participants to speak on topics of their choice within a particular thematic framework, it is noteworthy that several of the present essays interconnect in subject matter and approach. Indeed, the overall perspective here confirms the inter-disciplinary interests and practices that are increasingly typical of scholarship in the humanities today. From this perspective, the *Shāhnāma* of Ferdowsi offers an especially rich and fertile ground for intellectual interaction and complementary investigation among specialists in history, literature, and the visual arts and material culture, as the contributions to this volume attest.

The first set of essays here is by three experts in Persian literature and language. Olga Davidson extends her ongoing research on the so-called Bāysonghori preface to the famous *Shāhnāma* manuscript made for the Timurid prince Bāysonghor in 1430, and argues that the prefatory narrative reveals how the many (and oft-noted) textual variations and additions in books of the *Shāhnāma* evolved naturally from the process—what she refers

3. www.ilexfoundation.org

to as an *aetiology*—of reception and transmission in the oral and performative traditions of Ferdowsi's epic during the many centuries following its composition. Anna Krasnowolska also looks at the relationship between Ferdowsi's written and oral sources, using the love story of the Iranian hero Bīzhan and the Turanian princess Manīzha to examine how the poet incorporated selected *dāstāns* or "side stories," which may have originated as independent oral narratives, into the main flow of his epic. Firuza Abdullaeva considers another, much more fraught *Shāhnāma* romance, involving prince Siyāvosh and his step-mother Sudāba; she compares its historical origins, *femme fatale* theme, plot, and protagonists with the many and much better-known versions of the similar seduction tale of Yusof and Zolaykhā; and she draws on both literary and artistic evidence to explain how Ferdowsi came to be regarded as the author of a separate poem about Yusof and Zolaykhā.

The volume's second group of papers proceeds along interdisciplinary lines with reference to some of the same *Shāhnāma* tales and characters discussed by the other contributors. Historian Charles Melville compares the *Shāhnāma* story of Furūd, son of Siyāvosh, and particularly Ferdowsi's poetic account of the young hero's death, with various prose histories of the pre-Islamic kings of Iran in order to tease out the extent to which Furūd's own behavior leads to his tragic demise. Marianna Simpson, an art historian, considers medieval representations related to the by now familiar stories of Furūd and of Bīzhan and Manīzha on medieval Persian objects and in architectural monuments with the goal of assessing both the cultural context and the purpose of such epic imagery. Finally, Sumil Sharma, whose research interests meld Persianate literary and visual cultures, traces the history of *Shāhnāma* manuscript ownership and production as well as the emergence of *Shāhnāma* imitations and abridgements in early modern India in order to achieve a more thorough understanding of the interest in and cultural impact of Ferdowsi's epic during the Mughal period.

The editors bring this preface to a close by expressing sincere appreciation, on behalf of all the volume contributors, to the K. R. Cama Oriental Institute for the opportunity to gather in Mumbai for such stimulating and productive exchanges on Ferdowsi's incomparable *Shāhnāma*. This thousand-year-old masterpiece from Iran, with all its literary and artistic presence, promises to resonate world-wide for millennia to come.

Olga M. Davidson
Marianna Shreve Simpson
Boston and Philadelphia, August 2013

Interweavings of Book and Performance in the Making of the *Shāhnāma* of Ferdowsi

Extrapolations from the Narrative of the So-Called Bāysonghori Preface

Olga M. Davidson

Introduction

There is a wealth of evidence for the importance of live performances in the transmission of the *Shāhnāma* of Ferdowsi. This evidence is to be found in the material culture of the medieval Persian manuscript traditions themselves.

In making this point, I will rely in part on the dynamic new research emanating from the Cambridge *Shāhnāma* Project, as well as from a related publication edited by Robert Hillenbrand.[1] As we learn from various chapters in this volume, especially the one written by Shreve Simpson, there was a collaborative relationship between scribe and painter in producing illustrated versions of the *Shāhnāma*: the scribe copied out the text by hearing it dictated to him, while the painter painted illustrations that were thematically relevant to what was being dictated.[2] The thematic variations visible in the paintings can be matched with thematic variations in the textual transmission by way of dictation.

This paper focuses on recent research concerning the relationship between transmission and reception in oral poetic traditions and seeks to show, using specific examples, that variations in the textual transmission of the *Shāhnāma* can be explained in terms of variations in oral transmission. For some time now, as Simpson points out, art historians who specialize in the fourteenth-century manuscripts of the *Shāhnāma*, with all their textual variations, have appreciated such an explanation: "Interestingly, efforts by literary historians to place the *Shāhnāma* in the context of oral poetics and production do happen to coincide with tentative suggestions made by art

1. Hillenbrand 2004.
2. Simpson 2004.

historians some time ago when confronted with the range of textual variants in fourteenth-century illustrated volumes of [Ferdowsi's] epic."[3]

The stakes are high. When it comes to "investigations of the oral aspect of the *Shāhnāma*" as undertaken by myself and others, Simpson notes that they "have not been without their detractors," since "they seem to undermine [Ferdowsi's] role as the author of an original, written text."[4]

The Argument

In pursuing the topic of book and performance here, I will concentrate on a single manuscript of the *Shāhnāma*, the so-called Golestān *Shāhnāma*, produced in Herat for the Timurid prince Bāysonghor, son of Shāhrokh, in the year 833/1430.[5] The preface to this manuscript, as I argue, gives an extended narrative that motivates the actual production of the manuscript and illustrates how oral traditions that shape the composition of the *Shāhnāma* of Ferdowsi are interwoven with the concept of an "authoritative book" as the basis for authorizing any performance of any part of the *Shāhnāma*. My argumentation is linked with other previously published discussions that study the narrative of the Bāysonghori Preface as an example of narrative traditions centering on the Life of Ferdowsi tradition, and that compare the Bāysonghori narrative with other such analogous narrative prefaces to the *Shāhnāma* of Ferdowsi.[6]

An Inventory of Relevant Passages

In what follows, selected passages and paraphrases from the Bāysonghori Preface are linked with commentary that shapes the argumentation.[7]

At {366}, at the very beginning, the author of the Preface praises all the

3. Simpson 2004, 10.

4. Simpson 2004, 10.

5. There is an incisive discussion of the manuscript's historical and art historical background in Hillenbrand 2010.

6. Davidson 2001, 2008. The major "Life of Ferdowsi" narratives can be found in Riyahi 1993. The present discussion is part of a projected book in which I provide a commentary on the entire text of the Bāysonghori Preface to the *Shāhnāma* of Ferdowsi (as also on the texts of two other such prefaces), along with a translation in collaboration with Mohsen Ashtiany. See Hillenbrand 2010 for a reference to an earlier phase of this project. All the translations provided here stem from that larger project.

7. The numbers enclosed in braces indicate the pagination of the text as edited by Riyahi 1993. For example "{365}" indicates the page-break where p. 364 stops and where p. 365 begins. Each passage will be preceded by its corresponding initial page number of the original text as edited by Riyahi 1993.

four Caliphs: Abū Bakr, Omar, Othman, and Ali, thus registering the fact that the court of Bāysonghor is Sunni. If this author had been a Shiᶜite writer writing for a Shiᶜite patron, there would have followed a long eulogy of ᶜAli, Amir-al Moʾmenin, and praise of his valor and heroic qualities, and perhaps a heroic episode or two. It may be noted, however, that the Caliphs are praised very briefly. And, as we shall see later, the author of the preface accommodates Shiᶜite reception as well. As we also will see, the narrative of the Bāysonghori Preface accommodates a wide range of reception and transmission for the *Shāhnāma*, including even Shiᶜites.

Such accommodation in the narrative corresponds to a comparably wide range of extra verses that we see being inserted into the actual text of the Bāysonghori *Shāhnāma*. The number of verses in the text of the Bāysonghori *Shāhnāma* is over 58,000. The deliberateness of such textual accommodation has led to the description of this text as a new recension.[8] The term "Bāysonghori Recension" is justifiable in that the added verses represent an ambitious attempt by the compilers of the text to include variants from a vast array of different Persianate regions. Furthermore, these variants provide historical evidence for the ongoing reception and the transmission of the *Shāhnāma* tradition.

What appears most remarkable about the Preface to the Bāysonghori text of the *Shāhnāma* is that its narrative aims to validate the different additional verses stemming from different regions by giving explicit details about provenience and about regional rivalries that center on different claims about provenience.

The mass of additional verses in the text of the Bāysonghori *Shāhnāma*, I argue, can be viewed as accretions that evolved organically during the lengthy process of reception and transmission in the oral and performative traditions of the *Shāhnāma* as epic poetry—traditions that spanned a wide range of different regions in the Persianate world. Thus, the narrative of the Bāysonghori Preface can be viewed as the multiform story of this reception and transmission—what I now propose to call an *aetiology*.

The following example shows how the nature of the Bāysonghori text itself is reflected in the narrative of the Bāysonghori Preface:

> {369}: When it came to Yazdgerd's reign, all those historical accounts had been preserved in his library but in no particular order. He ordered Dāneshvar the Dehqān—a senior figure at Madāʾin [= at the royal court] who combined courage with learning and wisdom—to organize a list

8. On the concept of "recension" as a systematic attempt on the part of an editor or a team of editors to produce an edited text that accommodates variants found in a variety of manuscripts, see Davidson 2001.

> of chapters and arrange them in order from the beginning of the rule of Kayomarth to the end of the reign of Khosrow Parviz. And whatever lacunae he found there he filled and appended by asking information from the learned and the Zoroastrian *mōbads*. And so a chronicle of sheer perfection and comprehensiveness was created.

In terms of the aetiology presented in the Bāysonghori Preface, then, the Sasanian phase of reception and transmission was confined to an archetypal book written in prose. In terms of this same aetiology, the turning of this prose text into verse was the genesis of the oral tradition.[9]

In this light, it is instructive to examine how the narrative of the Bāysonghori Preface handles the aftermath of the Islamic conquest...

> {369} When Saʾd b. Waqqās captured Yazdgerd's treasures and library, the chronicle was part of the booty which they presented to the Caliph Omar. He sent for a translator to inform him of the contents. He recounted parts of the book dealing with the codes of justice of the Pishdādian and other Persian dynasties and their wise decisions and sober measures. The Caliph Omar was most pleased with these and ordered them to be translated into Arabic. But other sections contained far-fetched and unworthy matter. When Omar heard [the passages dealing with] the beliefs of the Sun worshippers and fire worshippers and the codes of the Sabians and the story of Zāl and Simorgh and such like, he decreed that the book was not fit for study and scrutiny, for it bore an exact likeness to this world and this [material] world was not worthy of attention and care. "In what sense is it like this world?" they [his entourage] asked.

> {370} "You have heard the Prophet say," Omar replied, "that God regards this world so worthless that he has mixed the licit and the illicit in it. And in this book too, the lawful and the unlawful are mixed together; I mean true and false."

We see in the narrative here an explicit aetiological reference to the fact that the Bāysonghori *Shāhnāma* is accretive. As will become clear in what follows, the narrative imagines the text of the *Shāhnāma* as a work in prose only, which will have to be turned into verse in order to come alive as poetry.

Here we continue tracking the narrative about the era that followed the Islamic conquest:

> {370} Then came a time when in Khorasan, the Al-e-Layth dynasty

9. Davidson 2001, where I offer a detailed study of the mythology and poetics that drive this narrative about an archetypal book.

> came to power. Ya'qub Layth sent an envoy to India to fetch a text. And he ordered Abū Manṣūr 'Abd-al-Razzāq b. 'Abd-Allāh b. Farrokh [sic] who was his close confidant to have all that Dāneshvar the Dehqān had recited in the Pahlavi language translated into Persian, and to add to it all that had happened between the time of Khosrow Parviz until the end of Yazdgerd. Abū Manṣūr therefore commanded his own official Abū Manṣūr al-Ma'mari to prepare the book using this copy accompanied by four others: Baheh b. Khorasan from Herat, Yāzdān-dād b. Shāpur from Sistan, Mahuy b. Khorshid from Nishābur, and Shādān b. Barzin from Ṭūs. And in the year 360 [*sic*] Hejri they prepared the book and they made copies in Khorasan and Iraq.

As I also have argued elsewhere, this part of the narrative is a compressed variant of what we read in the so-called Older Preface.[10] The narrative goes further:

> {370} And because Sulṭān Maḥmūd had been {371} brought up in a Samanid milieu, in all matters he had held them up as his example and model. And he spent most of his time conversing on learned subjects. He was particularly an avid reader of the history of the pre-Islamic Persian kings and he wanted to perform some deed on this score which had never been done by the Laythians or the Samanids: he therefore decreed that it should be rendered into verse.

In terms of the narrative of the Bāysonghori Preface, now and only now does the impetus to versify the *Shāhnāma* finally emerge. The internal logic of the overall narrative, however, retains the assumption that poets have all along been composing in verse the stories taken from the Book of Kings. As I also argued in my previous work, the idea that a prose Book of Kings is the authority for the oral traditions about the deeds of these kings and the deeds of heroes is part of an overall aetiology embedded in the oral traditions of Persianate song culture.[11]

> {371} And some people give this version of how the book came into Mahmud's hands: A certain Khor Firuz from Fars who was of a royal lineage and a descendant of Anūshīrvān, was forced by events to leave his native Fars and go into exile. The whirling wheel of fate, the tyranny of destiny and his unruly and dark fortune finally landed him in the city of Ghaznain, the royal seat of that just and religious monarch [= Mahmud.]

10. Davidson 2001.
11. Davidson 2001.

The wording here indicates that, as far as the narrative of the Bāysonghori Preface is concerned, it was the West Iranian version that became the prose archetype, as it were, for the *Shāhnāma*. But there is a rival version that already exists in prose, acquired from Sistan, and the versifier for that version is meant to be ʿOnṣorī, as the chief court poet of Sulṭān Maḥmūd.

As the Preface puts it, in a mixture of verse and prose:

> {272} Those riders on the playing fields of Persian poetry / those monarchs on the thrones of culture,
>
> Had thrown upon the field the balls of eloquence / Watched by spectators viewing the sight.
>
> In the midst of all this debate and judgment / They received a scroll from the poet ʿOnṣorī,
>
> Like a pearl from the sea or a gem from a mine / He presented it to the King of the World.
>
> When the Sultan set eyes on that piece of poetry / He placed it as a precious pearl upon his ears.
>
> He waxed lyrical in its praise / And favored him [= ʿOnṣorī] greatly at a special audience.
>
> Thus decreed the great ruler / that ʿOnṣorī should turn the book [*Shāhnāma*] into verse
>
> ...
>
> "In the past few days they have brought a manuscript from Sistan containing material on the life and manners of past kings. And the Sultan has decided that the best of these stories should be turned into verse. That explains why such crowds and multitude of poets have assembled at the court. Today was the day that the poets were to bring their versified pearls and present them at court. And in the Sultan's discerning mind, 'Onsori's poem was found the most beautiful. He has instructed him to carry out the task."
>
> Khor Firuz emitted a long sigh from his heart ...
>
> ...
>
> "I would not have rested until / I had brought this book to his court."
>
> ...
>
> Because of his great desire to acquire this book, the Sultan

> commanded that Khor Firuz should be given audience. And he questioned Khor Firuz about the possibility of acquiring the book.
>
> ...
>
> A messenger of the Sultan reached Khor Firuz's place and gave the letter to his people. They rewarded him with many gifts and gave the book to him. The messenger brought back the book to the Sultan. Because of this, Khor Firuz was greatly favored and attained a high rank at the court.
>
> And then the Sultan chose seven stories from this Annals of the Kings (*Siyar-al-moluk*) and distributed them among seven poets so that each could turn a story into verse.

So the book from Sistan, mentioned earlier, is now replaced by the book originating from Fars, the homeland of Khor Firuz.

To paraphrase the continuing narrative: While the poets were trying their luck at court with different versified versions of the book, the young Ferdowsi comes to town in order to seek justice and refuge from enemies at home.

So, whereas the poets in the court of Mahmud are tied to the concerns of an individual ruler, Ferdowsi is represented as the universalized poet of all Persianate peoples. His universality is linked to the accretive universalism of the Bāysonghori Recension.

The Preface to the original Bāysonghori manuscript in Tehran includes a single illustration, which depicts Ferdowsi coming forward and being greeted by one of three poets in a beautiful landscape setting. That poet is presumably ʿOnṣorī. Meanwhile, the other two poets sit a little distance away conversing together and two young slave boys stand further away holding a wine vessel and cup.[12]

The corresponding story, as told in the narrative of the Bāysonghori Preface, is as follows:

> {381} While this was going on, Ferdowsi stopped and settled down in a garden in the vicinity of the town and sent someone to the town to let some of his friends know that he had arrived. He then did his ablution ritual before performing his religious worship. By chance the poets of Ghazni— ʿOnṣorī, Farrokhī, and ʿAsjadi—had decided to get away from their rivals and enjoy a gathering in that garden, each bringing along

12. There is a full-page reproduction of this illustration (Ms 716 folio 007v) available on the Cambridge Shahnama Project: http://shahnama.caret.cam.ac.uk/new/jnama/card/ceillustration:507134948.

> a pretty slave boy with him. When Ferdowsi had finished his prayers, he decided to join them for a while. When they realized this, the poets said to each other, "the presence of this dry-as-dust ascetic will ruin our planned jollities; it is incumbent upon us to get rid of him." One of them suggested that they should pretend to be hog-drunk and treat him roughly to make him go away. ʿOnṣorī vetoed this. Someone else said, "Let's each recite a half-line of a quatrain in a difficult meter and ask him to compose the fourth half-line to complete it. If he agrees, he can join the company; otherwise it will serve as a good excuse to get rid of him." When he reached them, they acknowledged his presence and explained the conditions to him.

A later passage in the narrative of the Bāysonghori Preface highlights another important point. In this passage, we see that the ongoing versification of the stories of the *Shāhnāma*, the authority of which is viewed as stemming from a prototypical Book of Kings, is drawn into a parallel with a never-ending search for ever more versions of such a book, stemming from various different regions of the Persianate song culture. The point about the stories of such searching for more and more versions stemming from such an archetypal book is that the search parallels the mentality of the Bāysonghori Recension, which seeks to accommodate as many different versions as possible in a quest to contain the sum total of the *Shāhnāma* of Ferdowsi.

The following passage may suffice to reinforce this point:

> {375} And it is also reported that when the news of the King's great desire for collecting this book became known, the ruler of Kerman was anxious to seek Sulṭān Maḥmūd's friendship and was in the habit of constantly sending him gifts and presents, and in that time in Kerman there was one Āzarbarin, a descendant of the Sasanian emperor Shāpur Dhuʾl-aktāf, who was forever engaged in collecting accounts of the Persian kings. The ruler of Kerman heard about this and sent his collection to Sulṭān Maḥmūd. Sulṭān Maḥmūd gave the envoy ample rewards and sent many a gift to the ruler of Kerman, and their friendly relations were much strengthened.
>
> And also in Merv, there was a person from the lineage of Sām the son of Narimān called Āzād Sarv. And he had accounts of Sām, Zāl, and Rostam, and he took his collection to Mahmud.

A final example demonstrates the universalism of Ferdowsi as expressed in the narrative of the Bāysonghori Preface, which is intended as an expression of the universalism of the Recension:

{389} A group of envious people were maligning Hakim Ferdowsi and accusing him of dabbling in philosophy and Ismaʿili (or Zaydi) and Moʿtazelite views and whatever defect that they could attach to him.

On the strength of these verses of his:

You cannot see the Creator / Do not therefore tire your eyes

They called him a Moʿtazelite; for on the surface, these verses imply that the direct sight (of God) is impossible; as declared in Moʿtazelite doctrines.

And because of these verses

Behold this chagrin-ridden Dome / from which pain and remedy both emanate

{390} Attribute abundance to it, as well as need / From it comes your downfall and misery and from it, your success and rise.

They said that he was a philosopher. For these lines maintain that whatever happens in the world is under the influence of the Spheres including pain and its remedy, and increase and decrease in one's fortune; and this is the religion of the philosophers who attribute all events to the working of the spheres.

And from these verses:

Neither does the passage of time exhaust it / Nor does all that pain and suffering affect it

Neither does it ever rest from perpetual motion / Nor does it seek a refuge in the way we do,

they concluded that these verses attempt to prove that the motions of the spheres and the condition of heavens will always remain the same, and no change will affect it, and this is the creed of Materialists (*dahriyān*).

And such verses from which Shiʿism (or Zaydi and Ismaʿilism) can be deduced, and there are many,

If you are eager to enter Paradise / Get close to the Prophet and to ʿAli.

If you take offense at these words, blame it on me / This is how things are and this is my creed and way.

And that is why they called him a heretical Shiʿite.

> And the intentions of the people of ill-will and malice in these lines of reasoning and deduction are clear: for it is impossible for a person to be a follower of Greek philosophy, as well as a materialist, a Moʿtazelite, and a heretical [Zaydi] Shiʿite (an Ismaʿili) all at once. For those who believe in the eternity of this world have no business in liking or disliking ʿAli and ʿOmar, and those who favor ʿAli above others do not believe in the eternity of this world and attribute events to one's destiny and not to the planets and spheres. These contradictions that have been found in his poetry are inherent traits in the very nature of poetry which operates metaphorically and not literally; and perchance the meaning brought out by the critics to which they refer and object was not intended by the poet and he had other things in mind, verily God knows best!

There is a wealth of further extrapolations to be made from this narratological treasure house that we know as the Bāysonghori Preface. For now, however, I simply conclude by saying that the examples I have given so far show clearly the multiformity of the traditions that were tracked in the narrative of the Bāysonghori Preface and that were faithfully reproduced in the actual text of the Bāysonghori Recension.

BIBLIOGRAPHY

Davidson, O. M. (2001), "Some Iranian poetic tropes as reflected in the 'Life of Ferdowsi' traditions," in: M. G. Schmidt and W. Bisang (eds.), *Philologica et Linguistica: Festschrift für Helmut Humbach*; Trier, supplement, pp. 1–12.

—— (2013a), *Poet and Hero in the Persian Book of Kings*, Boston.

—— (2013b), *Comparative Literature and Classical Persian Poetics*, Boston.

Hillenbrand, R. (2004), "New Perspectives in Shahnama Iconography," in: R. Hillenbrand (ed.), *Shāhnāma: The Visual Language of the Persian Book of Kings*, Burlington, VT, 1–7.

—— (2010), "Exploring a Neglected Masterpiece: The Gulistan Shāhnāma of Bāysunghur," *Iranian Studies* 43: 97–126.

Riyahi, M. A. (ed.) (1993), *Sar-chashma-hā-ye Ferdowsī shenāsī*, Tehran: Muʾassasa-yi Mutalaʿat va-Tahqiqat-i Farhangi.

Simpson, M. S. (2004), "Shahnama as Text and Shahnama as Image," in: R. Hillenbrand (ed.), *Shāhnāma: The Visual Language of the Persian Book of Kings*, Burlington, VT, 9–23.

Ferdowsi's *Dāstān*—An Autonomous Narrative Unit?

Anna Krasnowolska
Uniwersytet Jagielloński, Kraków

The *Shāhnāma* is an example of a large epic poem which most probably came into existence through the gradual unification and cyclization of separate mythological and heroic tales of different origins. This development assumingly occurred over a long time span, through a process of transmission, proceeding in two parallel channels—the oral and the written. The final shape of Ferdowsi's work seems to be the result of his own creative effort and invention, which included a critical approach to and a selective evaluation of the material he had inherited from his predecessors.

A chain of stories built on the same structural pattern, but of different size and various degrees of complication, form the skeleton of the whole mythological part of the *Shāhnāma*. These are the subsequent variants of a three-generation death-and-vengeance story, originating from a death-and-resurrection myth of nature.[1] Contrary to the traditional opinion that Ferdowsi's narrative is loose, one-layered, and mainly linear,[2] a close investigation reveals a considerable degree of internal coherence, structural complexity, and density. This is particularly noticeable in the mythological part of the *Shāhnāma*.

Apart from those sections of the text that contribute to the main plot, the poem includes a number of side stories (*dāstāns*) that do not belong to the mainstream narrative in a strict sense and that, apparently, had originally functioned as separate narrative entities. These side stories came from independent (possibly oral) sources and were secondarily incorporated into the body of the "royal" epic tradition.

Within the texture of Ferdowsi's *Shāhnāma* a number of such *dāstāns*, which can be treated from the structural point of view as separate narrative

1. Krasnowolska 1983, 1989.

2. The authors working on the *Shāhnāma* compare its composition to a thread, a string (Bertel's 1934, 103; Kowalski 1952, 38; Arberry 1958, 44), a chain (Kowalski 1952, 39; Rypka 1968, 159; Safa 1973, 214;), an endless ribbon (Starikov 1957, 517), and an endless arabesque (Kowalski 1952, 39).

units, have been inserted. A *dāstān* is singled out from the flow of the main plot through a sort of frame, formed by its own introductory and closing parts, and characterized by a clear, compact composition: a single-threaded, well-defined plot that develops from a beginning, through culmination, until the conclusion.[3] In the practice of oral transmission a *dāstān* can be presented during a single performance. Yet, within Ferdowsi's work such tales, while keeping their autonomy, have been, to some extent, integrated into the mainstream of the narrative in several ways.

The questions of the degree of integration of a *dāstān* into an epic whole, of the role of an individual author's consciousness in this process, and of the methods used by him for this purpose will be examined in this paper. The *dāstān* of *Bīzhan-o Manīzha*[4] will be used as an example. This *dāstān* may serve as a good illustration of how an originally independent textual unit functions within the body of Ferdowsi's broader narrative context.

The *dāstān* of Bīzhan and Manīzha, included by Ferdowsi in his *Shāhnāma* and unknown to other sources,[5] is believed to be one of the few continuations of Parthian court literature, which has been mostly lost. The names of its heroes bear witness to such an origin.[6] According to Mary Boyce: "Bēzhan o Manēzha [...] was probably by origin an independent romantic lay, known to Ferdowsi from an old Pahlavi (i.e., Mid. Pers.) book [...] and incorporated by him in the *Shāh-nāma*."[7]

Dāstān-i Bīzhan-o Manīzha, a love story of a young Iranian knight and a Tūrānian princess, shows the typical features of a separate *dāstān*. According to scholars who have performed a stylistic analysis of this *dāstān*, this could be Ferdowsi's juvenile work, completed before he had set about implementing his great epic project.[8] Due to its complete plot, the story can function as an autonomous narrative entity; it has been singled out from the flow of the surrounding epic narrative by the means of its framing parts, an introduction and a closing sequence.

In the introduction to the *dāstān* (BM vv. 1–37) Ferdowsi, in the first person and in lyrical verse explains how this section of his work came into existence and points to its source, which is different from those of the rest of the book. The text opens with a beautiful description of a dark night, during which the narrator cannot sleep and a woman (a wife or a slave), having

3. 'Abbasspur 1997; Piecuch 1992, 95–96.

4. "Dastan-i Bizhan-o Manizha" (BM), in Shāhnāma (Firdousi 1960–1970) 5: 6–85.

5. But see Manuchehri 1991, 86; Safa 1973, 177–178.

6. Nöldeke 1901, 137; Coyajee, 1939, 151–154; Yarshater 1983, 458–461; Khaleghi-Motlagh 1990, 316–317; Melville 2006, 75–76.

7. Boyce 2003, 167.

8. Safa 1973, 177; Melville 2006, 72.

arranged a makeshift wine-drinking session in the garden, recites for the narrator an old story, taken "from a Pahlavi book" (*az daftar-i pahlavī*, BM v. 36), asking him to put it in verse. What follows then is said to be Ferdowsi's rendering of her tale, in New Persian versified form.

The conclusion of the *dāstān*, as frequently in Ferdowsi's poems, consists of an extended reflection on the instability of the world and the perversity of fate (BM vv. 1304–1311), after which comes the announcement of the story that is going to follow next.

The story itself has a compact and neatly constructed plot, which can be summed up as follows:

> During a banquet given by the king Kay Khusraw for his knights, a group of envoys arrives from a place called Armān on the Irano-Tūrānian border (BM vv. 55, 62, 70), asking the king for protection against the plague of boars that is devastating their lands. The king promises a reward to anyone who will fight the monstrous animals. The only volunteer is young Bīzhan, the son of Gīv. In spite of the objections of Bīzhan's father, the king lets him go on this dangerous expedition, sending with him Gorgīn, an experienced warrior, as his guide. Bīzhan engages in a fight with the terrible boars, while his companion refuses to help. After a successful end to Bīzhan's single-handed action Gorgīn is ashamed of his cowardice. He plans to get rid of Bīzhan as the only witness to his dishonor, by telling him about a place nearby, across the Tūrānian border, where Manīzha, the daughter of the Tūrānian king, Afrāsiyāb's goes for a New Year picnic every spring. Bīzhan accepts the idea of going to Tūrān, finds the place where the ladies are feasting and observes them from a distance. He is soon noticed by the princess and invited to join the party. Bīzhan and Manīzha fall in love with one another at first sight and cheerfully spend some days together. When the time for her return to the city comes, Manīzha is unwilling to part with her lover. She puts him to sleep with a sleeping drug and has him secretly transferred to her apartments. Upon waking, Bīzhan is not very happy with the development, but stays in the harem. After some time, King Afrāsiyāb gains knowledge of the presence of a man in his daughter's residence and orders that it be searched and the intruder arrested and hanged. It is only due to the intercession of Pīrān, the Tūrānian army commander, that Bīzhan's punishment is changed to imprisonment in a deep pit, sealed with a heavy stone. Manīzha, chased from her palace, has to collect food for her beloved as a beggar.
>
> Gorgīn goes back to Iran without Bīzhan. He invents a story

> about Bīzhan's kidnapping by a demon transformed into a wild ass, but nobody believes him. The king puts Gorgīn in jail, while Bīzhan's family and friends desperately look for the young man. Finally the king, using his magical goblet on the Nawrūz day, spots the place of Bīzhan's imprisonment. Rostam is summoned for help and soon sets off in merchant's disguise, with a caravan of goods, for Tūrān. After entering the capital he contacts Manīzha, and through her sends Bīzhan a secret message. The rescue takes place at night. Manīzha lights a fire at Bīzhan's pit to show its location to the rescuers, Bīzhan is liberated from his dungeon and together with his beloved returns safely to Iran. On their departure the Iranians raid the palace of Afrāsiyāb and take many goods and Tūrānian hostages. Gorgīn participates in the expedition and is forgiven his misdeed.[9]

In Ferdowsi's work the story of Bīzhan and Manīzha has been placed within the center of the broad cycle of the Irano-Tūrānian wars, in retaliation for the death of Siyāvush. Siyāvush, the heir to the Iranian throne, was forced to seek refuge in Tūrān after a conflict with his father, Kay Kāvūs. There he was well accepted and married twice—to Pīrān's daughter, Jarīra, and to Afrāsiyāb's daughter, Farangīs—but soon was accused of conspiracy and was murdered on the order of his royal father-in-law.[10] Siyāvush's son, Kay Khusraw, who was born after Siyāvush's death and who grew up in concealment in Tūrān, was found and brought to Iran by Gīv, son of Gūdarz. As the new king of Iran Kay Khusraw started a long war against his maternal grandfather, Afrāsiyāb, in order to avenge his father. Gīv's son, Bīzhan, the hero of our *dāstān*, thus belongs to an aristocratic family that plays a decisive role in the events of the Great War, and in spite of his young age himself takes part in most of its events.

Within the text of the *Shāhnāma* the *dāstān* of Bīzhan and Manīzha is preceded by a chain of war episodes: the tragic story of Kay Khusraw's half-brother Furūd (which also is a *dāstān* in its own right),[11] and two heroic tales about the Iranians' encounters with two powerful allies of Afrāsiyāb: Kāmūs i Kushānī[12] and a Chinese ruler (*khāqan-i Chin*).[13] The text that immediately precedes *Bīzhan-o Manīzha* is another *dāstān* of a similarly independent character, namely Rostam's adventure with Akvān-dīv.[14] The story

9. For a more detailed summary of the story and the related illustrations see Melville 2006.

10. "Dastan-i Siyavush," *Shāhnāma* 3: 6–250.

11. "Dāstān-i Forūd," *Shāhnāma* 4: 32–114.

12. *Shāhnāma* 4: 115–207.

13. *Shāhnāma* 4: 208–300.

14. *Shāhnāma* 4: 301–314.

of the Twelve Champions (*Dāstān-i Davāzdah Rokh*),[15] which directly follows *Bīzhan-o Manīzha*, takes us back to the theme of the war proper.

The *dāstān* of Bīzhan and Manīzha stays somewhat apart from the heroic context in which it has been inserted, due to its romantic character and its fairy-tale atmosphere characteristic of Persian folk tales. Yet, in spite of its distinctness and its independent source of origin, it has been integrated into the mainstream story in several ways.

Space, Time, and Actors

The events of the *dāstān* have been located in a space whose topography is, generally speaking, the same as that of the mainstream narrative of the *Shāhnāma*, and of a similarly schematic and conventional character. The capital of King Kay Khusraw in Iran (unspecified), and the residence of king Afrāsiyāb in Tūrān (in BM v. 911, p. 62 said to be the city of Khotan), are the two opposite poles of this universe. In between there are vast steppes (*dasht*), the flourishing countryside across the Tūrānian border, where Manīzha and her companions feast in the open air, and the nearby woods of Armān,[16] devastated by the boars. A "Chinese wood" (*bīsha-yi Čīnestān*; BM v. 415, p. 32) is also mentioned in relation to the stone covering Bīzhan's pit. When Gīv travels to ask Rostam for help he crosses the river of Hīrmand and enters Rostam's country, Zābol. (This route is repeated many times, in both directions, by the protagonists of the epos.) Thus, the space in which the events of the *dāstān* occur is perfectly familiar to the reader/listener of the *Shāhnāma*.

The time of the story is specified in a similarly conventional way. The *dāstān* has been located in the middle of the cycle of wars with Tūrān. Nevertheless, the opening verses of the story of Bīzhan and Manīzha proper (vv. 38–43) refer the reader to the beginnings of Kay Khusraw's rule. This period is represented not as wartime, but rather as the peaceful time of a new beginning after the new king's enthronement which, in epic mythology, is a return to an ideal, primeval state of the World:

چو کیخسرو آمد بکین خواستن   جهان ساز نو خواست آراستن
ز توران زمین گم شد آن تخت و گاه   بر آمد بخورشید تاج شاه
بپیوست با شاه ایران سپهر   بر آزادگان بر بگسترد مهر

15. *Shāhnāma* 5: 86–234.

16. Identified with Armān or Zarmān in Samarqand district: Shahidi-Mzandarani, 1998, 42–43. See Ḥudūd al-ʿālam 1970, 352.

زمانه چنان شد که بود از نخست   بآب وفا روی خسرو بشست

...

چو بهری ز گیتی برو گشت راست   که کین سیاوش همی باز خواست
ببگماز بنشست یک روز شاد   ز گردان لشکر همی کرد یاد

> When Kay Khusraw came to execute his vengeance, he decided to arrange the world in a new way. The royal throne disappeared from Tūrān, the king's crown reached the sun. The celestial sphere favored the king of Iran, and showed its kindness to the noblemen. The time became as it was at the beginning (*zamāna chenān shod ke bud az nokhost*), it remained faithful to the king. [...] When a [large] part of the World acknowledged his rule, he conceived the revenge for Siyāvush. One day he sat down to wine drinking, together with the champions of his army ...[17]

The protagonists of the story, except for Manīzha, who appears in no other part of Ferdowsi's work, are the same persons as in the mainstream narrative; the roles and features ascribed to them generally conform to their characteristics and frequently refer to their previous records. Rostam, for example, plays his usual role of a superman and rescuer of the lost and imprisoned, as he had already in a number of preceding stories (see below). Gīv, sent to Rostam for help (this time acting in his own cause), repeats his function from *Dāstān-ī Sohrāb* as the king's envoy.[18] Afrāsiyāb and Pīrān show the same attitudes towards Bīzhan as they did towards Siyāvush, hostility and cautious friendship, respectively, with the difference that this time Pīrān arrives in time to prevent the execution of the young Iranian. Thus, the expectations of the reader, who awaits the tragedy to be repeated, are not realized.

In some instances new features are added to the heroes' profiles. The function of Gorgīn as a treacherous guide is not a permanent component of his image; in the mainstream story he acts as a brave and loyal Iranian knight. However, his name, a derivative from *gorg* (wolf), probably should be compared with that of Esfandiyār's treacherous guide, Gorgsār.[19] Another distinctive feature is that this is the only text of the *Shāhnāma* in which Kay Khusraw owns a miraculous, "world-showing" goblet (*jām-i gītī-namā,* BM vv. 577ff.), in which, on New Year's Day, he can see invisible things. This attribute of Kay Khusraw is, however, in conformity with his role as a charismatic ruler, underlined in other parts of the epos.

17. This and the subsequent passages are translated by the author.
18. "Dastan-i Sohrab," vv. 315–371, *Shāhnāma* 2: 194–199.
19. "Padeshahi-yi Goshtasp," v. 278ff., *Shāhnāma* 6: 84ff.

Direct Links to the Epic Context

Some references in the text of *Bīzhan-o Manīzha* directly connect its action with the flow of events in the main body of the epic narrative. Most importantly, the story takes place in the shadow of the death of Siyāvush and in the context of the subsequent war, to which allusions are made in the text, as we have already seen. Manīzha, like Siyāvush's wife Farangīs, is king Afrāsiyāb's daughter in love with an Iranian; hence the two cases are perceived in the text as parallel and comparable to one another. Several references to the story of Siyāvush are made, as shown below.

Manīzha, when sending her nurse to identify the young man watching her picnic from a hilltop, tells her (BM vv. 197–199, p. 19):

نگه کن که آن ماه دیدار کیست   سیاوش مگر زنده شد گر پریست
بپرسش که چون آمدی ایدرا   نیایی بدین بزمگاه اندرا
پریزاده ای گر سیاوشیا   که دلها بمهرت همی جوشیا

Look! Who is that [youth] like a moon, is it Siyāvush resurrected or a fairy (*parī*)? Ask him how did he come here, and wouldn't he join our party? [Ask him:] "Are you the son of a *parī*, or Siyāvush, for all hearts beat with love for you."

In order to comfort Gīv after the disappearance of his son, Kay Khusraw relates to him a prediction about his future wars with Tūrān (BM vv. 541–544, p. 40), in which Bīzhan is said to play an important role:

که ایدون شنیدم از موبدان   ز بیدار دل نامور بخردان
که من با سواران ایران بجنگ   سوی شهر توران شوم بی درنگ
بکین سیاوش کشم لشکرا   بپیلان سر آرم از آن کشورا
بدان کینه اندر بود بیژنا   همی رزم جوید چو اهریمنا

Such I've heard from the *mawbads* and the wise learned men, that soon I'll rush towards the country of Tūrān with my Iranian riders. I will move my army in revenge for Siyāvush, my elephants will trample that country. Bīzhan will take part in that war, he will fight fiercely like Ahrīman.

When Gīv implores Rostam for help, the latter assures him of his readiness, bringing to mind their common campaigns of the past (BM vv. 708–710, pp. 49–50):

چه مایه ترا نزد من دستگاه   بهر کینه گاه اندرون کینه خواه
چه کین سیاوش چه مازندران   کمر بسته بر پیش جنگاوران

You know how much I cherish you; you were present at each battlefield, in the vengeance for Siyāvush, or in Māzandarān, each time you were among those ready for fight.

Pīrān, when advising Afrāsiyāb against hanging Bīzhan, reminds him of the disasters caused by the murder of Siyāvush (BM vv. 379–883, pp. 30–31):

مکش گفتمت پور کاوس را   که دشمن کنی رستم و طوس را
کز ایران بپیلان بکوبندمان   ز هم بگسلانند پیوندمان
سیاوش که بود از نژاد کیان   ز بهر تو بسته کمر بر میان
بکشتی بخیره سیاوش را   بزهر اندر آمیختی نوش را
بدیدی بدیهای ایرانیان   که کردند با شهر تورانیان

Didn't I tell you: do not kill Siyāvush, for you will make Rostam and Tūs your foes? The elephants of the Iranians will trample our land, they will tear us apart. Siyāvush, who was of royal blood, was ready to serve you, and you killed him thoughtlessly, adding poison to nectar. Then, you saw the misfortunes caused by the Iranians, you know what they have done to the country of Tūrān.

Finally, Rostam, while addressing Afrāsiyāb after having liberated Bīzhan from his prison, refers to the murder of Siyāvush, and directly compares the two situations (BM, vv.1132–1133, p. 74):

رها شد سر و پای بیژن ز بند   بداماد بر کس نسازد گزند
ترا رزم و کین سیاوخش بس   بدین دشت گردیدن رخش بس

Bīzhan has been liberated from the fetters—one does not harm his son-in-law; your hostility towards Siyāvush was enough, it's enough of driving my Rakhsh to the steppes.

The vengeance for Siyāvush is not the only external context to which the text in *Bīzhan-o Manīzha* refers. One finds in this *dāstān* some references to Rostam's adventures in Māzandarān (cf. above, BM, v. 709), which occur in a much earlier part of the *Shāhnāma.*[20] The two situations are similar because of the underground place of incarceration of the missing person and because of Rostam's role as rescuer in both cases.

20. "Padeshahi-yi Kay Kavus va raftan-e u be Mazandaran," *Shāhnāma* 2: 76–126.

In his letter to Rostam asking him for help in rescuing Bīzhan, Kay Khusraw enumerates all his merits, in particular his expedition to Māzandarān and the rescue of Kay Kāvūs imprisoned in a cave by the White Demon—Dīv-i Sepīd (BM v. 625, 629, p. 44–45):

جهانرا ز دیوان مازندران   بشستی و کندی بدانرا سران
...
همه جادوانرا ببستی بگرز   بیفروختی تاج شاهان ببرز

> You have cleansed the world of the Māzandarāni demons, having cut off their heads; [...] all the sorcerers have been crushed with your mace, you have elevated high the crowns of the kings.

Rostam, when speaking to the king, reminds him of this event (BM 815–816, p. 56):

بکندم دل دیو مازندران   بفر کیانی و گرز گران
مرا مادر از بهر رنج تو زاد   تو باید که باشی آرام و شاد

> I have torn out the heart of the Dīv of Māzandarān,[21] with the help of the royal glory (*farr-i kiyāni*) and of my heavy mace. I was born from my mother in order to fight for you; you should stay safe and cheerful.

Moreover, in our *dāstān* there are some allusions to the story of Rostam and Akvān-dīv, which in Ferdowsi's text immediately precedes *Bīzhan-o Manīzha*. The enormous stone that seals Bīzhan's prison is said to be the same that had been thrown by Akvān-dīv into the sea, and then miraculously transferred by God's power to the Chinese Wood (*bīsha-yi Chīnestān*; BM vv. 414–15). The pit itself is compared to "Arzhang's pit" (*chāh-e Arzhang*; BM v. 416, p. 32), which is an allusion to the cave of another demon killed by Rostam during his expedition to Māzandarān.[22] Afrāsiyāb tells his brother Garsīvaz:

ببر پیل و آن سنگ اکوان دیو   که از ژرف دریای گیهان خدیو
فگندست در بیشهٔ چین ستان   بیاور ز بیژن بدان کین ستان
بپیلان گردون کش آن سنگ را   که پوشد سر چاه ارژنگ را
بیاور سر چاه اورا بپوش   بدان تا بزاری بر آیدش هوش

21. This is an allusion to his tearing out of the liver of Div-i Sepid, whose blood alone could heal Kay Kāvūs's blindness caused by the Demon's sorcery ("Padeshahi-ye Kay Kavus...," v. 597, *Shāhnāma* 2: 108).

22. "Padeshahi-ye Kay Kavus...," vv. 520–525, *Shāhnāma* 2: 104.

> Take the elephants and, for the sake of Bīzhan, bring that stone of Akvān-dīv which God had brought out from the depth of the sea and thrown in the Chinese Wood. With the help of draught elephants bring that stone which closes the cave of Arzhang, and block with it the entrance of Bīzhan's pit, so that in penance he will come to reason.

References to Akvān-dīv and the Chinese Wood (*bīsha-yi shahr-e Chīn*) recur when Rostam, with his superhuman strength, opens Bīzhan's prison (BM vv. 1078–1079; 1085–1086, p. 71):

چو آمد بر سنگ اکوان فراز   بدان چاه اندوه و گرم و گداز
چنین گفت با نامور هفت گرد   که روی زمین را بباید سترد
...
ز یزدان جان آفرین زور خواست   بزد دست و آن سنگ برداشت راست
بینداخت در بیشهٔ شهر چین   بلرزید ازان سنگ روی زمین

> When he stood over Akvān-dīv's stone, at that pit of sorrow and misery and suffering, he said to his seven famous knights that the surface of the Earth should be swept away [...]. He implored the Creator of Soul for strength, he stretched his hands and simply lifted up that stone and threw it back to the Chinese Wood, so that the Earth shook.

In his adventure with Akvān-dīv, Rostam is carried in the air by the demon on a stone, and then thrown in the sea (Ad, v. 78: IV, p. 306), but we are not told about the further fate of the stone. The allusion in *Bīzhan-o Manīzha* seems to refer to a detail of the story, absent in the version recorded in the *Shāhnāma*. A wood of similar name: *bīsha-yi Shīrchīn* (*bīsha-yi shīr-i Chīn*: 'Wood of the Chinese Lion'?) or *bīsha-yi shahr-i Chīn* 'Wood in the Chinese country' is mentioned in reference to Kay Kāvūs's adventure, as the place in which the king fell on the earth with his flying throne, after an unsuccessful attempt at reaching the heavens (Hāmāvarān, v. 413).[23]

Gorgīn's invented version of Bīzhan's disappearance, for which he blames a demon transformed into a wild ass (*gūr*) (BM vv. 495–502, p. 37), seems to be inspired by the preceding story of Akvān-dīv in which a demon, having taken the shape of a beautiful wild ass (Ad vv. 25–30, pp. 302–303), leads Rostam astray and then carries him in the air.

The final battle with the Tūrānians, which ensues after the liberation of Bīzhan, fully integrates the story into its mainstream context: the rescue

23. "Razm-i Kay Kavus ba Shah-i Hamavaran," *Shāhnāma* 2: 153.

expedition changes into a plundering raid on the Tūrānian king's residence and thus, into one more of many episodes in the long war of retaliation.

The story of *Davāzdah Rokh* which follows next, as a continuation of the sequence of Irano-Tūrānian confrontations, is bound, through some allusions, to the preceding tale of Bīzhan and Manīzha. It begins with a reference to Rostam's attack on Afrāsiyāb's quarters and the latter's desertion (DR, vv. 20–21):

ازان پس که بر گشت زان رزمگاه   که رستم برو کرد گیتی سیاه
بشد تازیان تا بخلخ رسید   بننگ از کیان شد سرس ناپدید

After having returned from that battle in which Rostam had turned the world black for him, [Afrāsiyāb] rushed to Khallokh,[24] and he concealed himself from the [Iranian] kings (*Kiyān*), out of shame.

Afrāsiyāb plans an expedition against Iran, which, within the general plan of Ferdowsi's epic narrative, is another stage of the feud that broke out after the assassination of Siyāvush, but its direct cause is Afrāsiyāb's humiliation by Bīzhan and Rostam (DR, v. 44):

سپه خواست کاندیشهٔ جنگ داشت   زبیژن بدان گونه دل تنگ داشت

He called his army for he planned a war; in a way he felt offended by Bīzhan.

In this way an autonomous *dāstān* has been inserted within the main current of epic events, and "hooked" to it on both sides: by its referring to the events of the preceding parts of the poem, and its own events, in turn, being made a point of departure for the developments to follow.

Homogeneity of Building Material

The parallelism of the constitutive elements common to the *Bīzhan-o Manīzha* narrative and to the other (both mainstream stories and side stories) of the *Shāhnāma* is striking. This is due to the repetitive structural patterns and to the typological homogeneity of the building material of the epos as a whole. Such parallelisms contribute to the thickening of the entire texture of the poem, and binding its particular (not necessarily neighboring) parts tight to one another through a network of internal, inter-textual correspondenc-

24. Khallukh or Qarluq, a Turkish tribe of Altai; see *Ḥudūd al-ʿālam* 1970, 286ff.

es. Here are the most important motifs shared by the *dāstān* of Bīzhan and Manīzha and other parts of the *Shāhnāma:*

- The motif of falling in love with a princess of a strange and/or hostile ("demonic") country who seduces the hero, connects the text with the stories of Zāl and Rūdāba[25] and Rostam and Tahmīna.[26] In all three cases this is a girl who takes decisive steps in winning her partner. Moreover, seduction by a woman in a paradise-like garden in the middle of a desert is common to this story and to Rostam's and Esfandiyār's adventures with a witch during their subsequent *haft khwān* expeditions.[27]
- The imprisonment of the suitor by the girl's father likens this story to that of Kay Kāvūs and Sūdāba[28] in which the king of Hāmāvarān is an analogue of Afrāsiyāb from Bīzhan's adventure. The motif of a father's hostility towards his daughters' suitors (being in fact a part of their trial of initiation) is found in the story of Farīdūn's sons' marriages to the princesses of Yemen.[29]
- Gorgīn's role as a treacherous guide supplying false information to the hero places this *dāstān* within a series of stories in which the role of a guide (either honest or treacherous) is crucial. Thus, Gorgīn in this function can be compared to Rostam's guide Awlād (in his *haft khwān*), to Esfandiyār's guide to Rūyīn-dezh (Gorgsār),[30] as well as to Sohrāb's and Furūd's guides in the scenes of watching the Iranian army from the city walls in their subsequent *dāstāns*.[31]
- The faintly marked motif of Gorgīn's usurpation and his use of boar's tusks as a proof of his credibility (BM vv. 133, 208, 493, 553, 557) refer us to the exploits of Goshtāsp in Rūm, where the dragon's teeth play a similar, although much better developed, role.[32]
- The imprisonment of Bīzhan in a pit and Rostam's expedition in search

25. "Dastan-i Zal-o Rudaba," Manuchehr vv. 289–1464, *Shāhnāma* 1: 155–235.

26. "Dastan-i Sohrab," vv. 15–111, *Shāhnāma* 2: 170–177.

27. "Padeshahi-yi Kay Kavus...," vv. 395–424, *Shāhnāma* 2: 97–99 and "Dastan-i haft khwan-i Esfandiyar," vv. 175–232, *Shāhnāma* 6: 176–180.

28. "Razm-i Kavus ba Shah-e Hamavaran," *Shāhnāma* 2: 127–168.

29. "Padeshahi-yi Faridun," after v. 162, *Shāhnāma* 1, annex (Molhaqat V), 254–256.

30. "Padeshahi-yi Kay Kavus...," vv 474–879, *Shāhnāma* 2: 101–124; Dastan-i haft khwan-i Esfandiyar," vv. 32–431, *Shāhnāma* 6: 168–191.

31. "Dastan-i Sohrab," vv. 526–638, *Shāhnāma* 2: 211–219; „Dastan-i Forud," vv. 495–533, *Shāhnāma* 4: 40–43.

32. "Padeshahi-yi Lohrasp," vv. 553f.f, *Shāhnāma* 6: 42.

of him parallels the imprisonments of Kay Kāvūs by the White Dīv and by the king of Hāmāvarān, as well as the disappearance of Kay Kāvūs after his unfortunate flight to heaven, and Rostam's expeditions in his rescue, and also to Esfandiyār's quest for his sisters, imprisoned in Rūyīn-dezh (*Haft khwān-i Esfandiyār*).

- In more general terms, the *dāstān* of Bīzhan and Manīzha shares the motif of an expedition in search of a lost or concealed person with the stories of Farīdūn,[33] Kay Qobād,[34] and Kay Khusraw in exile.[35]
- The motif of entering a stronghold in disguise compares this *dāstān* with the stories of the conquests of Dezh Sepand by Rostam[36] and Rūyīn-dezh by Esfandiyār, as well as with Ardashīr's victory over Haftvād's worm,[37] which already belongs to the semi-historical part of Ferdowsi's work.

This enumeration, probably incomplete, shows how many stereotyped elements contribute to the composition of this particular story and how many parallel motifs attach it to the main body of the text and to its other side stories.

The preceding examples demonstrate the ways in which an autonomous side story, apparently staying outside the mainstream plot of the epic narrative, becomes integrated into its texture, thus contributing to the density and complexity of its general structuring.

As can be seen, this occurs in three basic ways:

- Through the placement of the mainstream and the side story within the same space and time of action and through the assignment of the same cast of protagonists. Heroes well known to the reader/listener, places and events of the mainstream story, together with their most typical features and attributes, reappear in the secondary *dāstān*.
- Through numerous references, allusions to, and interweavings with the main plot, which make a story function as an integral part of a larger epic narrative universe, and play defining structural roles in the composition of the whole. The events occurring in a secondary story may not definitively change the flow of events in the primary one, but by adding meaningful details and circumstances to the main

33. "Zahhak," vv. 230-245: *Shāhnāma* 1: 64-65.
34. "Padeshahi-yi Garshasp," vv. 112-206, *Shāhnāma* 2: 56-61.
35. "Dastan-i Siyavush," vv. 3021f.f, *Shāhnāma* 3: 198ff.
36. "Manuchehr," after v. 1617, *Shāhnāma* 1: annex (Molhaqat X), 266-272.
37. "Padeshahi-yi Ashkaniyan," vv. 694-749, *Shāhnāma* 7: 150-153.

plot action, they contribute to the building of the atmosphere and psychological premises of further events.

- Through structural means, in the sense that the compositional principles and building materials of the story are in keeping with those of the mainstream textual level; that is, they are composed of the same narrative elements as the main story plot. Such motifs as an initiation trial, a quest for a woman or a rescue expedition, a fight with a monster or strong adversary, which built the backbone of the main story, are here repeated and used in a parallel manner. The "grammar" of the story, i.e. the way in which these elements are put together into a compact structure, is common for the whole of the text.

A repertoire of the structural and textual elements inherent to the epic material that Ferdowsi had at his disposal had been formed in the long process of oral and then (or parallel to it), written transmission and gradual cyclization. As for the final version of the epic text, it was the author's role to make use of its internal possibilities in his literary construction, arranging these building elements into purposed, clear, and cogent compositions. If we assume that Ferdowsi had written the *dāstān* of *Bīzhan-o Manīzha* prior to the rest of his poem, then we have to accept that later on he would have adjusted it carefully to the context in which he decided to place it.

In Ferdowsi's work one can notice a very conscious effort toward giving coherence to his text by using the structural possibilities offered by the material at his disposal. Repetitiveness and homogeneity implemented in innumerable narrative variants gives the author an opportunity to structure his text in regular and somewhat rhythmical sequences. By juxtaposing similar, but not identical, narrative patterns he can escalate tension and build up expectation and suspense, leading to different solutions. In the case of *Bīzhan-o Manīzha*, the point of reference is double: on the one hand, a series of "rescue expedition" stories with their happy endings, on the other hand, *dāstān-e Siyāvush,* which ends with the hero's death. Knowing this the reader/listener may expect a tragic conclusion, which does not occur. Even more inter-textual correspondence based on the diversity and different development of similar patterns occurs between such pairs of *dāstāns* as *Haft khwān-i Rostam* and *Haft khwān-i Esfandiyār*, or *Dāstān-i Sohrāb* and *Dāstān-i Forūd.*

Besides the repetitive structural elements of one story, which refer the reader to another, similar one, there are in Ferdowsi's texts verbal references and allusions (usually placed in the mouths of the protagonists) that function as direct links between the particular parts of the poem. They seem to be, in reality, the author's own voice, showing clearly his control over the text.

The question of the author's creative consciousness as manifested, overtly or covertly, within his work—a question deserving serious investigation—reveals a different aspect of the orality versus textuality problem, namely the categories of inherited versus authorial, including the ways in which a "traditional" author constructs his own text out of the existing material.

Bibliography

'Abbaspur, H. (1997), "Dastan-i manẓum," in: H. Anusha ed., *Daneshnama-yi adab-i fārsi* II, Tehran, 579.

Arberry, A. J. (1958), *Classical Persian Literature*, London.

Bertel's, Y. E. (1934), "Ferdovsi i ego tvorchestvo," in: V. P. Volgin, B. V. Legran eds, *Fredovsi 934-1934*, Leningrad, 97–119.

Boyce, M. (2003), "Gōsān," *EIr* XI: 167.

Coyajee J. C., Sir (1939), *Studies in the Shāhnāmeh*, K. R. Cama Oriental Institute Publication no 33, Bombay.

Firdousi, (1960–1970), *Shākh-nāme. Kriticheskiy tekst* 1–9, red. Y. E. Bertel's, Moscow.

Ḥudūd al-ʿālam (1970), tr. and comm. by V. Minorsky, London.

Khaleghi-Motlagh, Dj. (1990), "Bižan," *EIr* IV: 316–317.

Kowalski, T. (1952), *Studia nad Šāh-nāme* I, Cracow.

Krasnowolska, A. (1983), "The Quest for immortality in the Šāh-nāme," in: M. Galik ed., *Proceedings of the Fourth International Conference of the Theoretical Problems of Asian and African Literatures*, Bratislava, 288–293.

—— (1989), "Elementy stylu epiki ustnej w *Šāh-nāme* Ferdousiego (Elements of Oral Epic Style in Ferdawsi's *Shahnama*)," in: A. Czapkiewicz ed., *Poetyka orientalna i jej recepcja w Europie*, Cracow, 137–154.

Manuchehri Damghani (1991), *Divan*, ed. M. Dabirsiyaqi, Tehran.

Melville, Ch. And F. Abdullaeva (2006), "Text and image in the story of Bizhan and Manizha: I," in: *Shahnama Studies I*, ed. Ch. Melville, Cambridge, 71–96.

Nöldeke, Th. (1896–1904), "Das iranische Nationalepos," *Grundriss der iranischen Philologie* 2, herausg. W. Geiger, E. Kuhn, Strassburg, 130–211.

Piecuch, M. (1992), "Epicka struktura 'Dāstān-e Sohrāb', jednej z ksiąg irańskiego eposu 'Šāh-nāme' Ferdousiego" ("Epic structure of Dastan-i Sohrab, one of the books of Ferdawsi's 'Shāhnāma"), in: T. Cieślikowska ed., *Problemy teoretyczne związków literatur i sztuk Orientu i Zachodu*, Cracow, 95–100.

Rypka, J. (1968), *History of Iranian Literature*, ed. K. Jahn, Dordrecht.

Safa Z. (1973), *Hamasa-sarayi dar Iran*, Tehran.

Shahidi-Mazandarani, H. (1998), *Farhang-i Shahnama. Nam-i kasan-o jayha*, Tehran.

Starikov A. A. (1957), "Firdousi i ego poema 'Shakhname'" ("Ferdawsi and his poem 'Shahnama'"), in: Firdousi, *Šaxname* I, transl., ed. C. B. Banu, A. Lahuti, A. A. Starikov, Moscow, 459–592.

Yarshater, E. (1983), "Iranian National History," *CHI* 3(1), 359–480.

The Legend of Siyāvosh or the Legend of Yusof?[1]

Firuza Abdullaeva
University of Cambridge

New Persian literature in its Golden Age had two versions of a similar story: one of native Iranian origin (Sudāba and Siyāvosh of Ferdowsi's *Shāhnāma*), and one with a Semitic background (Zolaykhā and Yusof of the Bible and the Qor'an and their later interpretations). However, having been introduced as haute/court poetry, the *Shāhnāma* version never received its continuation in the works of later authors, while the Qor'anic variant gave birth to a whole chain of emulations, including one that, since the early Middle Ages, has been attributed to Ferdowsi as well.[2] Why was the native story replaced by an alien version? And why has a telling of the story of Zolaykhā and Yusof that "rivals" an episode from the *Shāhnāma* been ascribed to the authorship of Ferdowsi? This paper intends to offer some answers to these questions, along with some background thoughts.

The story of a femme fatale tragically falling in love with a young man from her husband's household is well known in world literature from its earliest examples in different cultural milieus: from ancient Egyptian, Hellenistic, and Buddhist to later European traditions,[3] from the Far East to the extreme North and the Americas.[4] However, these typologically similar models have many variations in mythology, folklore, and authored literature. Euripides' *Hippolytus* (428 BCE) and later classical drama gave birth to the cross-cultural tragic image of Phaedra, the heroine who is a victim herself of universal female divine malice, as represented in literature, drama, visual art, and music. Interpretations of Phaedra have been produced in all European languages, including Marina Tsvetaeva's short play (1927), Thomas

1. I would like to thank Karen Lawson of the Royal Collection and Laila Galal Rizk of the National Library and Archives of Egypt for their kind assistance with obtaining the images for this publication.

2. An interesting psychoanalytical merging of both pre-Islamic and Shi'i traditions can be seen in Simin Daneshvar's earliest novel, *Sū va Shūn/Sāvushān* (*Persian Requiem*), published in 1969 (Krasnowolska 1999, 91–99).

3. Yohannan 1968; Abdullaeva 2012.

4. The database of Yu. Berezkin, included in my bibliography below, lists these versions; I thank Victoria Kryukova for bringing this useful resource to my attention.

Mann's dramatic novels (1936), and the latest opera by Hans Werner Henze (2007). Biblical tradition does not give the name of the woman married to the head of the Pharaoh's guards: she is more like a collective metaphor of a sinful and evil man-eater rather than a realistic image, as was so colorfully presented by Andrew Lloyd Weber in his *Joseph and the Amazing Technicolor Dreamcoat* (1968/2005).

In the Qor'an this story, to which a special *Sūra* is dedicated (12), is told almost in full, unlike most of the episodes in the Qor'an. However, it seems that the name of Zolaykhā, rather than simply "Potiphar's wife," started to be mentioned only in rather late *Midrash* (*Sefer haYashar*) tradition. In some Qor'anic exegetic sources Zolaykhā is called Rā'īl, suggesting an identification with Rāḥēl/Raḥel/Rachel, Joseph's mother.[5]

In the Islamic period the story received a wide range of interpretations, in which Zolaykhā varies from a ruthless and immoral seductress,[6] to a saintly virgin with a strong Sufi character.[7] These interpretations betray the ancient intercultural communications, including Persian, Parthian, and Greek traditions, which produced a great variety of versions, as was brilliantly demonstrated by V. Minorsky and D. Davis.[8]

The earliest surviving written evidence of this story seems to be an Egyptian tale of two brothers, Anpu and Bata, and Anpu's unfaithful wife, preserved in the *Papyrus d'Orbiney* (1185 BC).[9] This tale was obviously compiled from two or more sources. Its first part is about an unsuccessful attempt at the seduction of the younger brother, Bata, by Anpu's wife. The second part contains a myth about Bata (later represented as a female deity) who castrated himself and lost his masculinity, while becoming simultaneously a husband and a son of the woman, who is aggressively hostile towards him. The origin of this legend could go back to the belief in the demonic nature of women and their special connection with the demonic world,[10] which

5. Al-Tha'labī 1960, I, 332; Al-Tha'labī 2002, 148–185, Merguerian-Najmabadi 1997, 494; Stowasser 1994, 50–56; Brooks 1995; Renard 1996, 256–272.

6. Some exegetes, for example Nasīr al-Dīn Ṭūsī, even prohibited women from learning this story, as it was considered as unacceptable as drinking alcohol (Ṭūsī 1978, 219; *Nasirean Ethics* 1964; Merguerian-Najmabadi 1997, 501).

7. Jāmī 1337/1958.

8. Originally presented at the University of California, Los Angeles in April 2001, published later (Davis 2002; see also Minorsky 1964, 151–200).

9. *Papyrus D'Orbiney* (P. Brit. Mus. 10183), written ca. 1185 BCE; acquired by the British Museum in 1857 (*Egyptian Tales* 1895).

10. Some *Shāhnāma* manuscripts, like the Great Mongol (1330s; see Grabar and Blair 2008, 38–39), or the Ibrahim Sultan (1430–1435; Abdullaeva and Melville 2008, 117) give a revealing interpretation of the scene illustrating Iskandar seeing the Talking Tree. According to Ferdowsi, the tree had male and female human heads instead of fruit. The female heads could

could be chronologically attributed to the period of radical change, when matriarchate societies were replaced by social organizations with men in the dominant roles. A Dungan tale about the wife of the emperor's son could be a reflection of the female demonic element in this tale model.[11]

In many versions of the legend a malicious wife kills, or tries to kill, her old husband to free his space for her young beloved, who rejects her. These elements of murder and false accusation of the beloved exist in Greek novels, like Xenophon's *Ephesiaca* (ca. second century BCE), where the main hero, called Habrocomes, similarly to Joseph/Yusof, is sold into slavery in Egypt and whose master's wife, Cyno, unsuccessfully tries to seduce him. After being rejected she kills her husband, thinking that Habrocomes' motivation was his fear of him. However, Habrocomes flees, terrified by the prospect of sleeping with the ugly murderess. Later he is captured, and she accuses him of killing her husband.[12] Queen Sudāba also mentions her husband's death when she is trying to seduce Siyāvosh, implying that she might help in his succession to the throne.

The strategem of accusation is present in Jāmī's story (1468–1475) but in a reverse way: in a state of highest desperation Zolaykhā threatens to kill herself so that Yusof would be accused of killing her:

زلیخا گفت کای عبری عبارت   که بردی سخن وقتم بغارت
مزن بر روی کارم دست رد را   که خواهم کشتن از دست تو خود را
نیاری دست اگر در گردن من   شود خون منت حالی به گردن

You and your Hebrew ways of talking! You are wasting my time with your pointless talk!
Do not slap the face of my affair with the hand of your refusal, as I shall kill myself with your hand!
If you do not slip your arms around me in embrace, my death will be hung upon your neck![13]

The elements of murder and false accusation are already present in the story of Bata, which in later versions became separated into the one of

---

speak only at night, the male ones spoke during the day. The artist of the Ibrahim Sultan copy treated the scene in a rather imaginative way: he depicts a night scene when a female head speaks surrounded by her equals: dragons, beasts, and demons.

11. According to Berezkin's database, in a Dungan tale an emperor's son unknowingly married a daughter of the White Fox demon, who at night turned herself into a white fox and drank the blood of her husband's horses; when revealed by her husband's brother she accused him of raping her.

12. Xenophon 1957.

13. Jāmī 1958, 682; Jāmī 1980, 85.

the old husband and his son, in which Bata castrated himself. This story is related to the archetypal myth about the life-death-rebirth deities and semi-deities that is connected with the rituals of annually reviving nature and reflected in such images as Egyptian Anpu (Anubis > Osiris), Greek Adonis/Dionysus, Semitic Jesus, or Iranian Siyāvosh. However, female deities with similar functions seem to be their precursors: the evidence of the cults related to Akkadian Ishtar go back to 4000 BCE and Greek (or maybe Cretan) Persephone[14] to 1400–1200 BCE (or perhaps 1700 BCE).

By the Islamic period the collective image of an evil seductress found its place in the literatures of the Muslim world in a special genre of adventurous travelogue, usually as a frame story like the *Sindbadnāma* or the *Thousand and One Nights*. Female protagonists in these tales continue the Qor'anic idea of women with guile:[15] cunning and lustful creatures, whose only aim is to torture, seduce, and destroy the defenseless male population.[16]

New Persian literary tradition has its own story with a similar plot, which can be traced back to the earliest Iranian epic of Khwarazm (ca. 1300 BCE),[17] and was later incorporated into the *Shāhnāma*-style folk chronicles and into Ferdowsi's *Shāhnāma* in particular. For whatever reason,[18] apart from this, not many literary monuments have survived in written form before or even contemporary with Ferdowsi, although we know about their existence: Rudakī's *Story of Sindbad* and *Kalīla and Dimna* have not survived, nor have the three poetic romances written by 'Onṣorī, famous not as a novelist but as a great panegyrist. However, the titles of these romances, containing a male and a female name each, suggest that they were love stories about *Vāmiq and 'Azrā*,[19] *White Idol and Red Idol*, and *Shādbahr and 'Ayn al-Hayyāt*.[20] It seems that in these early works, already authored, but rooted in multicultural folklore, the standard image of a malicious femme fatale departs from this cliché and presents a long gallery of various romantic and relatively positive female portraits, especially those of Parthian origin, like Gorgānī's Vīs and Ferdowsi's Manīzha.[21]

14. Etymologically Persephone's name can be related to *Persia* and could be influenced by the intercultural contacts with the Iranians at the pre-Greek level.

15. On female sexuality in Muslim culture identified in the *Qor'an* as guile (*Qor'an*, *Sūra* 12 '*Yusof*' > Arab. *kayd al-nisā'* = Pers. *makr-i zanān*), see Merguerian-Najmabadi 1997, 485–508.

16. See, for example, Nisābūri's quotation, "One of the *'ulama'* said that he feared women more than Satan because, according to the Qor'an, Satan's cunning is weak (4:76) whereas women's cunning is enormous" (12:28) (Al-Nisaburi, 101). Cf. Dyaghilev-Benois' interpretation of the story in the libretto of the ballet Sheherezade (Paris, 1910).

17. Starikov1993, 574; See also Dyakonov 1951, 137–154; Tolstov 1948, 202–205.

18. Huyse 2006, 410–414; Davidson 2013a, 42–56.

19. For more detail see Hagg and Utas 2003.

20. Bertels 1988, 8-201; Huyse and Fouchécour 2006.

21. Minorsky 1964, 151–200; Abdullaeva and Melville 2006, 71–96.

In 1908 Hermann Ethé published in Oxford his critical edition of the poem *Yusof and Zolaykhā* based on five known manuscripts and two lithographs. He was the most convinced supporter of the theory ascribing the authorship of the poem to Ferdowsi. Ethé's prominent Cambridge colleague, E. G. Browne, expressed the same opinion in his *Literary History of Persia*, published in 1902. Even by the time of E. E. Bertels, who relied mostly on the analysis of A. T. Tagirdjanov,[22] this theory managed to survive the first attempts of M. Mīnovī to demolish it.[23] Now *Yusof and Zolaykhā* is known as a work that was probably written by a court poet called Amānī or Shamsī, who composed it for his Saljuq patron, Shams al-Dīn Ṭogānshāh b. Alp Arslān, in exchange for releasing the poet from a prison pit "like Yusof."[24]

According to those who ascribed this poem to Ferdowsi, he wrote it so as to rehabilitate his name and reputation as a true Muslim in Baghdad, where he had fled from the anger of Sulṭān Maḥmūd via Tabaristan. There, according to another legend, he wrote a killing satire on the Ghazna ruler, after which he could not expect anything but painful death. However, both of these "facts" mentioned in the different anthologies are now disregarded as beautiful legends created by court poets who were using Ferdowsi's example to preach to their patrons how they should treat them and their fellow litterateurs.[25]

The name of Ferdowsi, like that of, for example, Shakespeare, is surrounded by so many legends, old and modern, that some suggest that even his existence could be a legend.[26] I have no doubt that Ferdowsi did live in the tenth-eleventh century and that he did write his poem, *Shāhnāma*, having spent the last thirty or so years of his long life on it, and finished it on 8 March 1010.[27] "His" *Yusof and Zolaykhā* was supposedly written to rehabilitate his reputation by writing a poem on the Qor'anic subject, applying the usual method of *javāb* (Pers. 'answer')/*nazīra*/*tazmīn* (Arab. 'imitation/emulation'), which meant the inevitable improvement of the work of his

22. Tagirdjanov 1948.

23. There is a late 1970 reprint of Ethé's Oxford edition of 1908 (*Yûsuf and Zalîkhâ* 1970), see also Bertels 1960, 232.

24. Mīnovī 1944, 49–68; Nafisy 1950, 41, 53–54; Tagirdjanov, 1948. For full bibliography see De Blois 2004, 476–482.

25. The earliest surviving version of this legend of 1156–1157, in Nizāmī 'Arūzī Samarqandī's *Chahār Maqāla*, is already fully shaped (Nizāmī 'Arūzī Samarqandī 1376/1997, 77–86; Nizāmī 'Arūdī Samarqandī 1899).

26. We do not consider new, groundless theories, based on the assumption that Ferdowsi's *Shāhnāma* is a product of a collective work of several editors, who lived throughout the thirteenth through eighteenth centuries (Nosovskiy-Fomenko 2010).

27. Abdullaeva and Melville 2010, 1–11. On the dates of Ferdowsi's life see Omidsalar 2012, 108–109.

predecessor. However, this poem does not present as much "improvement" of the original ideas as Jāmī's version.

Jāmī's *Yusof and Zolaykhā*

The improvement of the Qor'anic story, which was told in great detail in a special *Sura Yusof*, was quite a tricky task. However, despite the ambiguities, this was not an obstacle for many writers and poets who undertook to elaborate the Qor'anic legend, from Ṭabarī's sober version [28] to the Sufi super-erotic romance by Jāmī.[29]

It was not Jāmī who first turned a traditionally sinful, lustful, and mendacious woman into a saintly virgin, communicating with angels in her dreams. He was obviously following some of the existing mystical interpretations of the story: the transformation had occurred long before, when al-Qoshayrī (986–1072) chose to describe Zolaykhā as a prime example of preferring another to oneself, or Sohrawardī (1155–1191) who, in his tale about the three brothers Beauty, Love, and Sorrow, associated Zolaykhā with Love.

In Jāmī's interpretation she has a more important role than that of the prophet Yusof:[30] it is she who sees prophetic visions and dreams. It is she who undertakes a long spiritual journey (*tarīqa*) full of obstacles and hardships, physical and moral, and reaches her beloved. In the beginning, driven by desire, she builds a palace and tries to take Yusof through its seven doors, locking each of them after he enters with an iron lock and a gold chain; but he flees. She falsely accuses him, repents and loses everything she once had: her wealth, youth, beauty, idols, and gods, even her eyesight, all for the sake of her love for Yusof. She eventually marries him and spends the rest of her happy life with Yusof, producing children and having grandchildren. In the end of her first stage she loses her earthly sight in order to be able to witness the divine miracle and regains it to see Yusof again. In the end of the story she blinds herself again, in order to be able to regain divine sight after her physical death.

28. However, even this narrative is full of intriguing details, witnessing that Yusof desired Zolaykhā and was about to have intercourse with her ("he sat between her legs, loosened his garment, sat with her as a man sits with his wife, etc.") but suddenly saw a divine sign on the wall or ceiling, after which "he was sore afraid, and his lust went out of him by the tops of his fingers" (Ṭabarī 1969, 16: 33–49).

29. On different surviving versions of this poem see Dadbeh 2009.

30. This idea is probably reflected in the *hadīth* that states that Yusof was detained for five hundred years at the gates of paradise and not admitted so that the pollution of worldy kingship might be fully removed from him (Razi 2003, 228).

Yusof Fleeing from Zolaykhā, Saʿdī, *Bustān*, Behzad, Herat, 1488, Cairo, The National Library and Archives of Egypt, 22, Adab farsi 908.

Jāmī gives powerful and contrasting descriptions of the last moments of both personages: Yusof dies quietly in his bed, surrounded by his family and disciples. Zolaykhā's last monologue is as powerful and disturbing as Ophelia's song and Romeo's last monologue ("Eyes, look your last!"): she comes to Yusof's grave with exhausted soul and mind and talks to his spirit and body hidden underneath the earth. Having reached the peak of her exaltation she tears her eyes out of their sockets and plants them into the soil as if they were narcissus bulbs, saying: "What use are eyes to me in a garden bereft of the sight of your face?!"[31] and dies going to paradise, where she will see her Yusof again. How different is this vision compared with, for example, Dante's scene from the Fourth Zone of the Eighth Circle of Hell, assigned to the Falsifiers of Words, where Potiphar's wife wanders eternally like a shadow, punished for her malice and lies.

Although Jāmī is the last giant of the Golden Age of Persian classical literature, his powerful work inspired several later authors, up to the eighteenth century: one of the latest versions, based on Jāmī's interpretation was produced by Āzar Bīgdelī (d. 1780).

Yusof and Zolaykhā Published by H. Ethé

The *Yusof and Zolaykhā* story published by Ethé has a rather traditional interpretation of the legend: it is a story of Yusof, in which Zolaykhā's role is very secondary, almost marginal.

It is clear that the author, whoever he was, was a talented poet, which explains why Ethé and other prominent colleagues were prepared to identify him with a mature Ferdowsi. The following episode, in which Yusof as a little, orphaned boy is auctioned at the slave market is one of many powerful scenes:[32]

که خرد غلامی چو سرو سهی نکویی ورا خوبی و خسروی
که خرد غلامی چوباغ بهشت که با او بیامد رخ حور زشت
که خرد غلامی که نزدیک و دور دهد روی او همچو خورشید نور

Who will buy a boy who is like a tall cypress tree, who has goodness and beauty and kingly grace!
Who will buy a boy who is like the garden of Paradise, next to whom the Hurī would look ugly!
Who will buy a boy whose face spreads light to near and far like the Sun!...

31. Jāmī 1958, 727; Jāmī 1980, 135.
32. *Yûsuf and Zalîkhâ* 1970, 272, 274.

که خرد غلامی یتیم و اسیر   که کس نیستش در جهان دستگیر
که خرد غلامی ذلیل و غریب   که کس نیستش مر درد او طبیب

Who will buy a boy—an orphan and captive, who has nobody in the whole world?
Who will buy a boy humble and alien, who has nobody to cure his pains?...

Despite its obvious merits, it is difficult to imagine that this poem could belong to the same author as the *Shāhnāma*. However, Ethé and his followers were convinced by such indications in the poem as the following *bayts*:[33]

بسی گوهر داستان سفته ام   بسی نامه باستان گفته ام
ببزم و برزم و بکین و بمهر   یکی از زمین و یکی از سپهر...
دلم سیر گشت از فریدون گرد   مرا زان چه کو تخت ضحاک برد
گرفتم دل از ملکت کی قباد   همان تخت کاوس کی برد باد

I have pierced enough of the pearls of tales, I have said enough of the old stories
About feasts and battles, anger and love, one about earth and one about heaven ...
I am fed up with the knight Farīdūn; what is the profit for me that he took the throne from Zahhāk?
I have turned my heart from the kingdom of Kay Qobād and from the throne of Kay Kāvūs, which has gone with the wind ...

Indeed if these lines were written by Ferdowsi they witness the greatest tragedy the poet could have ever survived: the betrayal of the work and the credo of his whole life.

Obviously, the poet who wrote these lines wanted to introduce a much better story compared with all others in Ferdowsi's *Shāhnāma*. However, the story he told used the same model Ferdowsi already had in his poem.

Ferdowsi's Sudāba and Siyāvosh

This story in the *Shāhnāma* is one of the most important: Ferdowsi's Siyāvosh is full of obvious and hidden symbolism, maybe hidden even from Ferdowsi himself,[34] and follows the known Middle Persian sources.[35] Ferdowsi is not

33. *Yûsuf and Zalîkhâ, 1970*, 23–24.

34. Dyakonov 1951.

35. *Bundahishn* XXXIII 10, see Rak 1997. As O. Davidson has shown in the case of the story of Siyāvosh, Ferdowsi gives a direct reference to the oral narrator after whom he was writing down this *dāstān* (Davidson 2013b, 24–26).

absolutely clear about Siyāvosh's rather enigmatic origin.[36] The name of his mother, who was found in the bushes (!) by three noble knights, is not known. She explained her strange position in the bushes by the fact that she had run away from her drunken father, who was a descendant of king Farīdūn (while her mother was a descendant of Garsīvaz); however, she had no material evidence of her noble origin except her beauty: all her possessions, including her horse, had been stolen by ruthless robbers. Her noble beauty impressed the three noble knights, and each of them wanted to have her for himself. Eventually they decided to kill her to save their friendship. At this decisive moment a wise man suddenly emerged and suggested they take her to the king. Having seen her, Kay Kāvūs immediately made her his queen.

In the spring she gave birth to the loveliest baby, who was called Siyāvosh. Shortly afterwards Rostam asked the king to give him the boy so that he could take him to Zabulistan and train him in all the aristocratic skills of the chivalric code (*bazm* and *razm*, 'feasting' and 'fighting'), in which Rostam so excelled. Many years passed before Siyāvosh asked him to let him see his father. For Rostam, Siyāvosh had become a cure for his souring mental wound, on whom he had poured all his unrealized paternal love which had suddenly been awakened in him when he had killed his own son, Sohrāb.[37] Ferdowsi masterfully describes how the feeling of guilt piled up in Rostam's mind: when he kept lying to Sohrāb during their battles and especially when he could not be with Sohrāb during his last minutes. Lying on the royal brocade, the dying Sohrāb. looked around trying to find his father among those who crowded around him and closed his eyes forever, while Rostam was on his way to Kay Kāvūs to ask for the elixir which could revive Sohrāb. The refusal of the king to save his son Sohrab enormously affected Rostam's loyalty towards the king, and one can presume that Prince Siyāvosh was inevitably influenced by this disloyalty from his early childhood.

As was mentioned by Davis, Siyāvosh had many fathers and none at the same time.[38] Among all Siyāvosh's fathers, including his real one and his fathers-in-law, Pīran and Afrāsīyāb, Rostam was the one who contributed most to his education and the formation of his personality, one of the main features of which was that he was more interested in manly deeds than in women and family. Being aware of Rostam's power over supernatural crea-

36. Siyāvosh/Siyavakhsh < Syāvaršan ('with black hair/horse', or 'the one who possesses horses with black manes', cf. Hippolytos' hippophoric name which is almost a calc of Siyāvosh, see: Russell 1988, 47–53) in *Gosh Yasht* IX 18, 22; *Ard Yasht* XVII 38, 42, in Rak 1997, 369, 370; *Zamyad Yasht* XIX 77, Rak 1997, 397. Cf. Zaratushtra < 'the one who possesses old camels'.

37. For more on this see Davidson 2000, 128–142.

38. Ferdowsi 1992, xxiii.

Gīv, Tūs and Gūdarz discover a beauty in the bushes, Firdawsī, *Shāhnāma,* 1648, Mashhad, The Royal Collection © 2011, Her Majesty Queen Elizabeth II, Ms Holmes 151 (A/6) f. 132r.

tures, Sudāba later accused Siyāvosh of using sorcery learned from his tutor for his miraculous survival of the fire ordeal.[39]

The role of Siyāvosh's own mother is reduced to an absolute minimum,[40] and it seems that she was not asked if her son could be taken from her by Rostam. She dies unnamed when Siyāvosh is appointed the ruler of Transoxiana. He alone mourned her for a month, until the knights who had brought her to the court, Ṭūs, Gīv, and Gūdarz, managed to console him. It is uncertain where she was by the time of her death: it is very probable that she preferred to move to Siyāvosh's castle, trying to escape from the jealous intrigues of Sudāba, similar to those of Shīrīn regarding Maryam. Maybe Siyāvosh even had some suspicions about his mother's early death and mistrusted Sudāba due to her possible involvement in it.

When Siyāvosh came of age the king declared Mawarannahr as his principality. This obviously correlates with the cult of Siyāvosh, which has been associated with Transoxiana, and with Khwarazmian and Soghdian[41] culture in particular. During its evolution the pagan nature of the ancient hero was absorbed by the Muslim tradition on the basis of the common idea of martyrdom. As a result of this synthesis the mystical sacrificial element became predominant and created a Jesus-like figure who readily accepts his execution, performing the role of a victim in a ritual sacrifice.[42]

The misfortune in Siyāvosh's horoscope, which was compiled at the moment of his birth, starts when Siyāvosh meets Sudāba, his father's beloved queen.

Sudāba is one of very few characters in Ferdowsi's epics who are depicted with more than just one color. The features of her character, which are so contrasting and contradictory, may suggest that Ferdowsi used more than one source to construct her image, or was inspired by the story so much that he raised his narrative to the level of Dostoevsky-like multidimensional psychoanalysis. A foreigner,[43] an Arab princess, the only beloved

39. Exactly like the protagonist Chariclea from Heliodorus' *Æthiopica*, who safely went through a fire ordeal to prove her innocence and was accused of sorcery: Heliodorus 1895; Davis 2002, 94.

40. She is introduced with the sole purpose of giving birth to Siyāvosh: some scholars suggest that Ferdowsi needed characters like Siyāvosh and his father in order to provide ancestry for Kay Khosraw (see, for example, Vevaina 2007, 231–243).

41. Among the most recent publications related to this see Morano 2009, 325–330.

42. The scene of the Execution of Siyāvosh with a compulsory depiction of a gold bowl to collect his blood during the decapitation was one of the most popular among the illustrators of the poem since the fourteenth century.

43. The etymology of this name is not entirely clear. It is possible that Sudāba is a result of the contamination of the Iranized Arabic *su'dā* (سعدی) and the Avestan *Sutawanhu*

daughter of the powerful king of Hāmāvarān (Ferdowsi's Yemen), she totally dedicated herself to her husband, the Persian king who invaded her country and forced her father to give him everything, including his wealth and his daughter. Despite her father's attempts to destroy Kay Kāvūs and bring her back she makes her choice and follows her husband to jail, where she shares with him all the calamities. Her determination to be with her beloved against her father's will is very similar to the behavior of the Turanian king's daughter Manīzha, who in the poem has a clearly positive character.

Apart from these two cases, Ferdowsi mentions several others in which fathers are desperately trying to keep their daughters in their household, while the daughters are trying their best to leave them, even if they know that they would be joining rather populous harems. For example, King Sarv tries to resist the marriage of all three of his daughters to Farīdūn's sons. This can be interpreted as a trace of the pre-Islamic arrangement of the Zoroastrian family, especially of royal descent, when fathers would be encouraged to marry their daughters to maintain the perfection of the lineage. Ferdowsi mentions this, even telling the story about the Arab kings, although such an arrangement had never been established. In any event, though Ferdowsi is not concerned about foreign wives spoiling the genealogy of Iranian kings, Siyāvosh is.

When Sudāba arrives in Iran she gets the status of the head queen in the harem, although this status could be changed any time, and Ferdowsi mentions at least once that she was dismissed and replaced by Siyāvosh's mother. To keep her position, the queen had to have enough influence on the king and be able to manipulate his mind, a skill in which Sudāba excelled. It is interesting that Siyāvosh refuses to marry one of his half-sisters, Sudāba's daughters because of her Arab origin. He states that they are "full of wiles and hatred for the Persian people."

To be fair, Siyāvosh was raised in a male-dominated environment and is disgusted by the whole idea of female company.[44] Despite her being the queen, the splendor of her appearance, and her seductive techniques, Fer-

(> *sūd* 'profit, usefulness'), while the NP *sūdāvar* 'profitable, useful' could give *sūdāva/Sudāba* (*Burhān-i Qāti'*, 676), which was later shaped according to the 'Rūdāba' pattern (Starikov 1993, 641). The fact that Ferdawsi identifies her as Arab by origin could be a reflection of the fact that the story had been borrowed from the western lands (Semitic, Greek, or Egyptian). Despite her very Iranian-looking name, Ferdowsi's Sudāba is an Arab princess due to her evil nature, which supports his main concept of nationalism and royalism. Ferdowsi's idea that only an Iranian and a royal by blood could be a legitimate ruler of Iran often conflicts in his narrative with the stories of Iranian kings having foreign mothers, and particularly in the case of Zahhāk, originally an Avestan serpentine evil character which in the *Shāhnāma* is turned to an Arab prince (Davis 2006, 117). For more on Zahhāk as a symbol of alienness, causing evil, or evil being brought by foreigners, see Schwartz 2012, 275–279, Omidsalar 2012, 138–144.

44. Abdullaeva 2010b, 108.

Siyāvosh fleeing from Sudāba, Firdawsī, *Shāhnāma,* 1648, Mashhad, The Royal Collection © 2011, Her Majesty Queen Elizabeth II, Ms Holmes 151 (A/6), f. 136r.

dowsi's Sudāba seems to be a bit older than Siyāvosh: in the harem she had several daughters of marriageable age whom she used as a pretext to have Siyāvosh in her quarters. Her last argument of persuasion, that he abused her sincerity when she opened her secret to him, could not be strong enough to overcome his fear or loyalty towards his father. Davis suggests that his resistance and integrity had "something of an anguished adolescent flight from sexuality about it."[45] I would add that Siyāvosh was still mourning the untimely passing of his mother, whose love he missed desperately, in contrast to which the lustful wiles of Sudāba could be particularly unacceptable to him.[46]

This is the moment when the woman in love turns to the woman in hatred and, like her many counterparts, fakes her beloved's crime: she accuses Siyāvosh of raping her and of causing the death of the king's twin babies, with whom she claims to have been pregnant. Despite having gone through the trial and being declared innocent Siyāvosh leaves Iran for Turan where he is falsely accused and executed. Immediately after he learns the tragic news of Siyāvosh's death, Rostam executes Sudāba in the royal harem. No protest is raised by the king. Sudāba herself accepts her death readily: she has no reason to live anymore. It is notable that despite his hatred towards this woman, Rostam does not plot her death. He kills her in a state of grief and with some respect for her status. Compare this with Kay Kāvūs, who during the investigation considered a humiliating execution by public hanging to show that Sudāba had lost her royal rank, while she insisted on decapitation.

What made Sudāba change her personality? What enflamed her immediate[47] passionate love towards her step-son, putting her reputation and life in danger? It could be Siyāvosh's irresistible beauty, causing Yusof-like *fitna*,[48] as E. Morano mentions in his comment on a phrase from the *Book of Giants*.[49] Ferdowsi, however, speaks extensively about the beauty and elaborate decoration of Sudāba and her court, but says nothing about Siyāvosh's appearance except that he had an angelic face. It is possible that Ferdowsi

45. Davis 1992, xix.

46. If we presume that as in the story of Shīrīn and Khusraw's head queen Maryam, Sudāba was somehow involved in the early death of Siyāvosh's mother, it would be possible to understand the disgust Siyāvosh felt towards her. We can also compare the story of Vīs (in Gorgānī's *Vīs and Rāmīn*) who refused to have any sexual relationship with her old husband, Mūbad, on the pretext that she was still mourning her father.

47. Compare this with Zolaykhā who, according to Ṭabarī, waited six years before starting to approach Yusof.

48. Tabari 16:133–146; Stowasser 1994, 53.

49. Morano 2009, 328, 330.

Rostam executes Sudāba, Firdawsī, *Shāhnāma,* 1648, Mashhad, The Royal Collection © 2011, Her Majesty Queen Elizabeth II, Ms Holmes 151 (A/6), f. 167r.

identifies Siyāvosh with Yusof and omits his description as pleonastic, since Yusof's beauty is well known without even mentioning it.

Yusof and Zolaykhā in Persian Poetry

As said above, despite the very psychologically elaborate presentation in the *Shāhnāma*, the story of Sudāba and Siyāvosh never gained popularity in later and even contemporary court poetry, having been replaced by the one about Zolaykhā and Yusof. Sufi poets, like Sanā'ī, 'Attār, and Rūmī, actively used these images in their mystical parables; for Sanā'ī, Khāqānī, 'Attār, Vakhshī, Nizāmī, Sa'dī, and Hāfiz this couple was already a common trope. Nāsir Khosraw suggests that his own propagandistic sermons can have the same miraculous effect as Yusof's prayer, which could restore the beauty and youth to Zolaykhā and cure the blindness of Yusof's father.[50]

The following are a few of the many *bayts* that demonstrate the extreme popularity of this imagery in classical poetry.

Rūmī (1207–1273) used the images of Yusof and Zolaykhā much more frequently than all other poets. In his poetry, too, Zolaykhā is given the main role of a suffering lover, while Yusof is only a 'trap' (*ghazal* 40):

چه داند دام بیچاره فریب مرغ آواره را
چه داند یوسف مصری غم و درد زلیخا را

What does a trap know about the miserable captive, the singing bird?
What does Egyptian Yusof know about the grief and pain of Zolaykhā?

Sanā'ī (d. 1131) reflects on the changing roles of the couple in one of his *ghazals* (235):

عاشق و معشوق و عشق این هر سه را در یک صفت
گه زلیخا گه نبی گه یوسف کنعان کنیم
روح باطن گر چو یوسف گم شدست از پیش ما
ما چو یعقوب از غمش دل خانهٔ احزان کنیم

The Lover, the Beloved, and Love: we attribute all these three
Sometimes to Zolaykhā, sometimes to the Prophet, sometimes to Yusof of Kan'ān

50. See more details in Dadbeh 2009; Prigarina-Averyanov 2003, 18–30; Prigarina 2008, 389–418.

If our inner spirit gets lost like Yusof
We, like Ya'qub will turn our heart to the house of grief.[51]

This fragment could have inspired Hāfiz to write his famous "Lost Yusof will come back to Canaan, don't grieve ..." (*Yusof-i gom-gashta bāz āyad ba Kan'ān gham makhor*).

In his *Bostān* (Chapter 9) Sa'dī (1184–1283/ca. 1291) gives his interpretation in the form of Zolaykhā's monologue addressed to Yusof, where the author offers a rather unexpected Khayyamic conclusion, "Don't waste your time while you are in this world, do not feel ashamed of your desires, you will regret if you leave them unfulfilled, enjoy life and repent when you still can," which seems to be contrary to the whole idea of the Qor'anic story.[52]

زلیخا چو گشت از می عشق مست
به دامان یوسف درآویخت دست

When Zolaykhā got intoxicated from the wine of her love
She grasped Yusof's hem...

تو در روی سنگی شدی شرمناک
مرا شرم باد از خداوند پاک
چه سود از پشیمانی آید به کف
چو سرمایهٔ عمر کردی تلف؟
شراب از پی سرخ رویی خورند
وز او عاقبت زرد رویی برند
به عذرآوری خواهش امروز کن
که فردا نماند مجال سخن

You became ashamed before a face of stone
Shame on me from the Pure God!
What profit is in your palm from regret,
When you waste the capital of your life!
People drink wine for the sake of getting a red face
But they get pale faces of death from Him.
Ask for forgiveness today,
There won't be a chance to do this tomorrow.

51. I thank Fereshteh Fletcher for her advice on this translation.
52. Sa'dī (n.d.), 436.

'Attār (ca. 1142–ca. 1220) in his *Manṭeq al-Tayr* offers a little interpolation to the episode when, rejected and enraged, Zolaykhā sends Yusof off to jail and orders her slave to whip him cruelly. When the slave sees Yusof naked he cannot bear to hurt such a perfect body and suggests that Yusof should scream as if he is beaten. However, in the end the slave decides that he must leave some traces on Yusof's body to avoid problems. When the slave gives him the real whip, Yusof sighs deeply instead of screaming. Having heard this very sigh, Zolaykhā orders the punishment stopped—her loving heart immediately distinguishes a sigh that was caused by real pain from many fake cries:[53]

چون زلیخا زو شنود آن بار آه
گفت بس، کین آه بود از جایگاه
پیش ازین آن آهها ناچیزبود
آه آن باد این ز جایی نیز بود

When Zolaykhā heard him sigh this time,
She said: Enough! Because this sigh came from somewhere[54] else.
Before this, those sighs were nothing!
Let that sigh be! As this one was from somewhere else too.

Awhadī (1271–1338) directly refers to the primary source of his imagery and speaks about what it means for him:[55]

پس بخوانند مقریان ز نخست
سورهٔ یوسف و زلیخا چست
تا ز قرآن کلاه و جامه کند
همه را محو عشق نامه کند

Then they will recite from the beginning
The enchanting *Sura* of Yusof and Zolaykhā
Until it will dress them from head to toes in the Qor'an
And this love story will annihilate everything.

Jāmī's version is a culmination of the intertextual evolution of the story

53. Farid al-Din 'Attār (1964), 77.
54. This could be a pun, as *jāyagāh* could be an epithet of 'heaven'.
55. Awḥadī 1983, 37.

from the Qor'an. The poet seems deliberately to have changed the details, as Nizāmī was doing with Ferdowsi's texts. For example, in the story about Bahrām Gur and his slave girl[56] Ferdowsi's "Noble" (Āzāda) Rūmī slave is turned into a Chinese "Troublemaker" (Fitna), rebelling against her name and destiny and marrying the prince like Cinderella instead of being killed by him. However, the most important of Nizāmī's mystical interpretation of Fitna's role is similar to the one of Yusof, who was a *fitna* (moral destruction) for Zolaykhā.

Similarly Ferdowsi's story of Khusraw and Shīrīn is reinterpreted by Nizāmī, who assigns to Farhād a more significant role than to either protagonist in Ferdowsi's version.

The story of Yusof and Zolaykhā could have originated in a pre-Biblical Mesopotamian milieu from a legal case of a mature noble woman trying to seduce a young slave or stepson in her or her husband's household. Her attempts to approach the young man could have been based on her frustration at not being the only wife in her husband's harem (Ferdowsi's version), or due to her husband's sexual incompetence (Jāmī's version). Despite her accusations of rape and the proof that the young man was innocent (the fire ordeal in the *Shāhnāma* and a speaking baby in *Yusof and Zolaykhā*) the guilty party was not punished.[57] For this reason this case could have entered the professional legal annals and become public and popular among the wandering storytellers who spread the old pre-Islamic folklore, among which there were not only Judaic and Christian legends.[58]

Ethé and all prominent scholars who supported him in ascribing *Yusof and Zolaykhā* to Ferdowsi could be right in their argument that the poet reached the peak of disillusionment propagating Iranian myths and memories, which had to compete rather unsuccessfully with those stories coming from a new Islamic layer of his native culture, especially after the disastrous reception of his poem. It does not matter much whether Farrukhī in the *bayt* below meant Ferdowsi's poem or any of his sources; the fact is that the

56. Meisami 1989, 41–75; Meisami 1995, 303–315; Meisami 2006, 48–52; Abdullaeva 2012, 41–44.

57. According to Hammurabi's code (ca. 1780 BCE) a virgin, if raped, was considered innocent, while married women and their attackers were considered equally guilty and would both be executed by being thrown in the river, although the woman's husband had the right to save her if he wished to do so. According to the Hittite Code of Nesilim (ca. 1650–1500 BCE) a man would be executed if he raped a woman at a distance from her house, but if he raped her within her house, she was deemed culpable and could be executed as well. It was assumed that the woman did not scream or show her resistance, bringing others to her rescue, and therefore she must have consented to have sexual intercourse (Smith 2004, 15).

58. Piotrovskiy 1991, 100.

genre of heroic epic was already out of fashion at the Ghazna court,[59] replaced by the most bombastic panegyric and entertaining lyric, produced in large quantities by the employees of Mahmud's state media and propaganda department.

همه حدیث ز محمودنامه خواند و بس
همانکه قصه شهنامه خواندی هموار

He who used to read the tales from the *Shāhnāma*
Is now reading only the stories from the *Mahmudnāma*[60]

By no means do I want to compare Ferdowsi with Ayatollah Khomeini, who turned from political speeches to erotic poetry imitating Sufi imagery of 'Attār, Rūmī, and Hāfiz, to fit the demands of the contemporary cultural milieu. However, it could be possible that the poet, having suffered the most severe lack of appreciation of his life's work, turned to the much more popular subject, which did not require any special effort to be introduced. And this could be the grounds, if not for accepting Ferdowsi's authorship of *Yusof and Zolaykhā*, at least for explaining the poem's attribution to him.

Conclusion

An ancient fertility myth that evolved into the universal story of a lover whose love turns to hatred when it is rejected is present in almost all known literary traditions. At the peak of its Golden Age, New Persian literature had two rival versions of the legend.

So why did Rudakī never mention the legend of Siyāvosh, whose cult had been practiced in Rudakī's land for centuries and was extremely popular in his time? Why was the legend of Yusof ascribed to Ferdowsi, similar as it was to the legend of Siyāvosh that he had already narrated in his *Shāhnāma*?

Rudakī and the Legend of Yusof

The legend of Ferdowsi arriving at the court of Sulṭān Maḥmūd and the competence test spontaneously organized in the garden by his colleagues 'Onṣorī, Asjadī, and Farrokhī, usually recounted in the prose preface of the

59. It is worth remembering Farrokhī's personal experience when he arrived in Chaghanian looking for a job at the local court and almost missed his chance at the interview with the chancellor due to his provincial-looking dress and turban (Nizāmī 'Arūzī Samarqandī 1997, 58–65).

60. *Farrokhī* 1371, 65; Bertels 1988, 205; Bertels 1960, 349; Abdullaeva 2010a, 20–21.

Shāhnāma manuscripts, indicates that nobody, not even well-versed and educated poets of Ghazna, knew the stories from the *Shāhnāma*. On the other hand, Rūdakī's audience would have been expected to recognize immediately the Zolaykhā story in the poems, like the powerful piece about the three shirts of Joseph, or the *bayt* below, in which the poet compares his heart, bleeding from love pain, with the hands of the Egyptian ladies witnessing the magic beauty of Zolaykhā's slave and cutting their hands instead of the oranges they were peeling:[61]

یوسف رویا کز او فغان کرد دلم
چون دستی زنان مصریان کرد دلم...

Oh Yusof-faced about whom my heart was crying
He made my heart [bleed] like the hands of the Egyptian ladies ...

There could be several reasons why Rudakī preferred to use the image of Yusof instead of Siyāvosh, among them:

- Rūdakī used the image of Siyāvosh but his writings referring to the Iranian version of the story have not survived.
- Rudakī was brilliantly educated in Arabic classical literature and, being a bilingual poet, was using Arabic literary imagery not only to demonstrate his knowledge and upbringing but as a habit.
- By the time of Rudakī a more multi-dimensional, mystical interpretation of the story, connected with the Qor'anic characters, became more popular among litterateurs than the rather archaic and straightforward tale of behavior motivated by "lust-fear" of the *Shāhnāma*. Authors would use a familiar story, recognizable in their cultural milieu but a different, more exoticized version to make it fresher and more attractive for the audience. Orientalism, as a trope, was heavily used already in Greek adventure romances, in which the protagonists or their environment would often be "Persianized" or "Egyptianized."
- The Zolaykhā and Yusof story was not always associated with an alien or new religion, as it could have penetrated Transoxanian folklore before Islam and through a different route: according to Narshakhī (ca. 899–959), at this time in Mawarannahr Islam was still not absolutely dominant.[62]

61. Rudakī 2007, 67.
62. Narshakhī 1351/1972–73; Narshakhī 1954.

Ferdowsi and the Legend of Siyāvosh

The following observations suggest why Ferdowsi might have included the Siyāvosh story in the Shāhnāma and also authored *Zolaykhā and Yusof*:

- Ferdowsi's attempt to revive the old Transoxanian legend of Siyāvosh was a deliberate act of his personal *sho'ubiya*, or nationalistic inclinations. Due to his heroic efforts it became possible to replant the ancient myth and cult of resurrecting nature from Mawarannahr ("behind the river [Oxus]") in the mainland of *Iran-zamin* and merge it with the idea of Shi'i martyrdom.
- For Ferdowsi, who had never been in Transoxania, the cycles of Siyāvosh and Rostam could carry the same exotic and attractive flavor of distant horizons, like Yusof for Rudakī, or Persinna and Hystaspes for Heliodorus.
- The need to produce a *nāsikh* Zolaykhā story to replace Ferdowsi's *mansūkh*[63] Sudāba original[64] was probably based on awkwardness related to some features of the pre-Islamic family structure, which were by this time perceived as socially and legally unacceptable, for example Sudāba's offer to her husband to marry their daughters to his son.[65] Otherwise the story of the ruthless femme fatale Sudāba is closer to that of Zolaykhā in Ethé's text than is Zolaykhā's image in the Qor'an to its rather ambiguous interpretation by Jāmī.
- The legend of the great poet betraying his life's work himself and conforming to circumstances was created in opposition to the unfair treatment of his genius by Mahmud.
- The consistent iconography of the scene of seduction both in illustrated manuscripts of Ferdowsi's *Shāhnāma* and in the versions of the Yusof and Zolaykhā story proves that the artists treated the episode as one and used an established cliché for it.

A brilliant example of contemporary art demonstrates vividly how easily such a merge could happen in the Middle Ages: a New York artist, Hamid Rahmanian, illustrating the English translation of the *Shāhnāma* in the technique of digital collage, re-used the visual elements of both stories, being

63. *Nāsikh* and *mansūkh*—terms of Qur'anic exegesis, literally meaning 'abrogating' and 'abrogated' respectively.

64. Burton 2012.

65. The prohibition against marrying one's sisters and more than one at a time is stated in *Sūra al-Nisā'* 'Women' (4:23). Compare the openly negative attitude in the Islamic milieu towards *Vīs and Rāmīn* with similar family arrangements.

Sudāba entertains Siyāvosh in her quarters. Digital collage, original in color. Copyright Hamid Rahmanian. Reproduced by courtesy of the artist.

unaware of their different provenance. His picture depicting Sudāba entertaining Siyāvosh in her dwellings preserves the fragment of the original illustration of the Egyptian ladies cutting their fingers instead of oranges, enchanted by the beauty of Yosuf when he was suddenly summoned by his mistress Zolaykhā.

A millennium ago Zolaykhā was more popular among poets and artists due to the collective cultural memory. Her fame has still not faded away. Sudāba came back from oblivion due to the fame of Ferdowsi and his single-handed efforts.

Bibliography

Abdullaeva, F. I. and Ch. Melville (2008), *The Persian Book of Kings, Ibrahim Sultan's Shāhnāma*, Oxford.

Abdullaeva, F. and Ch. Melville (2010), "Shāhnāma: the Millennium of an Epic Masterpiece," in *Iranian Studies, Journal of the International Society for Iranian Studies* 43/1: 1–11.

Abdullaeva, F. I. (2010a), "The Shahnameh in Persian Literary History," in B. Brend and Ch. Melville (eds.), *Epic of the Persian Kings. The Art of Ferdowsi's Shahnameh*, London and New York, 16–22.

—— (2010b), "Firdowsi: Male Chauvinist or Feminist?" in *Painting the Persian Book of Kings Today. Ancient Text and Modern Images*, edited by M. Milz, Cambridge, 102–120.

——— (2012), "Women in the Romances of the Shāhnāma," in *Love and Devotion: from Persia and beyond*, edited by S. Scollay, Melbourne, 41–48.

—— (forthcoming), "From Zolaykhā to Zuleika Dobson: Femme Fatale in Persian Literature and Beyond," in R. Hillenbrand, A. Peacock and F. Abdullaeva (eds.), *Ferdowsi, the Mongols and Iranian History: Art, Literature and Culture from Early Islam to Qajar Persia*, London.

Awḥadī Marāghah'ī (1983), *Dīvān-i kāmil*, edited by Amīr Aḥmad Ashrafī with preface by Nāṣir Hayyirī, Tehran.

Berezkin, Yu. E., *Thematic classification and distribution of folklore and mythological motifs according to geographical areas*, (database): http://starling.rinet.ru/cgi-bin/bdescr.cgi?root=/usr/local/www/data/berezkin&morpho=0&basename=\data\berezkin\berezkin. Accessed 21 July 2013.

Bertels, E. E. (1988), "Struggle of the Court Poets of Sultan Mahmud against Firdawsī," in *History of Literature and Culture of Iran*, Moscow.

—— (1960), *History of Persian and Tajik Literature*, Moscow.

—— (1988), "Hakim 'Unsuri from Balkh," in: *History of Literature and Culture of Iran*, Moscow, 8–201.

Burhān-i Qāti' (1336), edited by Muhammad 'Abbāsī, Tehrān.

Brooks, G. (1995), *Nine Parts of Desire. The Hidden World of Islamic Women*, London.

Burton, J. (2012), "Abrogation (Nāsikh wa Mansūkh)," *Encyclopaedia of the Qor'an*, edited by J. D. McAuliffe, Washington D.C., Brill online, 2012: http://www.encislam.brill.nl/public/abrogation#q3_id2748726.

Dadbeh, A., A. Keeler, and Ch. Kia (2009), "Joseph in Persian literature, Qur'anic exegesis and art," in *EIr online*: http://www.iranicaonline.org/articles/joseph.

Davidson, O. (2013a), *Poet and Hero in the Persian Book of Kings*, third edition, Boston.
—— (2013b), *Comparative Literature and Classical Persian Poetics*, second edition, Boston.
Davis, D. (1992), *The Legend of Seyavash*, New York.
—— (2002), *Panthea's Children: Hellenistic Novels and Medieval Persian Romances*, New York.
—— (2006), "The Aesthetics of the Historical Sections of the Shāhnāma," in *Shāhnāma Studies I*, edited by Charles Melville, Cambridge.
De Blois, F. (2004), *Persian Literature. A Bio-bibliographical Survey. Poetry of the Pre-Mongol Period*, 5, London.
Dyakonov, M. M. (1951), "Images of Siyavush in Central Asian Mythology," *Publications of the Institute of History of Material Culture* 40, Leningrad, 137–154.
Egyptian Tales (1895), translated from the papyri and edited by W. M. Flinders Petrie, illustrated by T. Ellis, London.
Farid al-Din 'Attar (1964), *Manṭeq al-Tayr*, edited by Ṣ. Gawharin, Tehran.
Farrukhi Sistani, Abul Hasan Ali ibn Julugh (1371), *Divan*, edited by M. Dabir Siyaqi, Tehran.
Ferdowsi (1992), *The Legend of Seyavash*, translated by D. Davis, London.
Grabar, O. and S. Blair (1980), *Epic Images and Contemporary History: The Illustrations of the Great Mongol* Shahnama, Chicago and London.
Heliodorus (1895), *An Aethiopian Romance, Englished by Thomas Underdowne*, revised and partly rewritten by F. A. Wright, introduction by Charles Whibley, London.
Hägg, Th. and Bo Utas (2003), *The Virgin and Her Lover: Fragments of an Ancient Greek Novel and a Persian Epic Poem*, Leiden: Brill Studies in Middle Eastern Literatures.
Huyse, Ph. and Ch-H. de Fouchécour (2006) "Iran III, Persian Literature (1–2) Pre-Islamic Literature and Classical Literature," in *EIr* XIII: 4: http://www.iranicaonline.org/articles/iran-viii1-persian-literature-pre-islamic. Accessed 21 July 2013.
Jāmī, Abd al-Rahman (1337/1958), *Masnavi-yi Haft Awrang*, edited by Aqa Murtaza and Mudarris Gilani, Tehran.
Jāmī, Nuruddin Abdurrahman (1980), *An Allegorical Romance: Yusuf and Zulaykhā*, translated by D. Pendlebury, London.
Krasnowolska, A. (1999), "Mytho-epic Patterns in Modern Persian Literature," in *Proceedings of the 3rd European Conference of Iranian Studies II*, Wiesbaden, 91–99.

Meisami, J. S. (1989), "Fitna or Azada? Nizāmī's Ethical Poetic," in *Edebiyat, A Journal of Middle Eastern Literatures* 2/1: 41–75.

——(1995), "An Anatomy of Misogyny?" *Edebiyat, A Journal of Middle Eastern Literatures*, N.S. 6, 303–315.

—— (2006), "Writing Mediaeval Women: Representations and Misrepresentations," in *Writing and Representation in Medieval Islam*, edited by Julia Bray, London and New York: Routledge Studies in Middle Eastern Literatures, 48–52.

Melville, Ch. with contributions by F. I. Abdullaeva (2006) "Text and Image in the Story of Bizhan and Manizha I," *Shāhnāma Studies I* (Pembroke Papers 5), edited by Ch. Melville, Cambridge, 71–96.

Menovi, M. (1944), "Ketab-e hazara-ye Ferdawsī va botlan-e entesab-e Yusof-u Zolaykhā ba Ferdawsī," *Ruzgar-i nau* V/3: 16–36.

Merguerian, G. K. and A. Najmabadi (1997), "Zulaykhā and Yūsuf: Whose 'Best Story'?" *International Journal of Middle East Studies* Vol. 29, No. 4: 485–508.

Minorsky, V. (1964), "Vis u Ramin: A Parthian Romance," in *Iranica. Twenty articles*, Tehran, 151–200.

Morano, E. (2009), " 'If They Had Lived ...' A Soghdian-Parthian Fragment of Mani's Book of Giants," in *Exegisti monumenta. Festschrift in Honour of Nicholas Sims-Williams*, edited by W. Sundermann, A. Hintze, and F. De Blois, *Iranica* 17, Wiesbaden, 325–330.

Nafisy, S. (1950), "Le Yusuf et Zalikha attribué à Firdowsy," *Archiv orientalni* XVIII/1–2: 351–353.

Narshakhī, Abū Bakr Mohammad b. Ja'far (1351/1972–73), *Tārīkh-e Bukhārā*, tashīh va tahsiyah-ye Modarres Razavī, Tehran.

—— (1954), *Tārīkh-i Bukhārā, The History of Bukhara*, translated from a Persian abridgment of the Arabic original by Narshakhī, edited and translated R. N. Frye, Cambridge, Mass.

Nasirean Ethics, English translated by G. M. Wickens, London, 1964.

al-Nisābūrī, Nezām al-Dīn al-Hasan b. Mohammad b. Al-Hosayn al-Qommī (n.d.), *Ghara'eb al-Qor'ān wa raghā'eb al-forqān*, 5, Cairo.

Nezāmī 'Arūzī Samarqandī (1376/1997), *Chahār Maqāla*, edited by M. Qazvīnī, Tehrān.

Nezāmī 'Arūdī (1899), *Chahār Maqāla, or Four Discourses*, translated by E. G. Browne, London.

Nosovskiy, G. V. and A. T. Fomenko (2010), *Shahname: Iranian Chronicle of the Great Empire of the 12th–17th Centuries*, Moscow.

Omidsalar, M. (2012), *Iran's Epic and America's Empire. A Handbook for a Generation in Limbo*, Santa Monica.

Piotrovskiy, M. B. (1991), *Qor'anic stories,* Moscow.
Prigarina, N. I. (2008), "Beauty of Yusof in the Mirrors of Persian Poetry and Miniature Art," in *Indologica, Festschrift in memoriam T. Ya. Elizarenkova, Orientalia et Classica* XX, Moscow, 389–418.
Prigarina N. I. and Yu. Averyanov (2003), "Disappearing Beauty of Yusof," *Vostochnaya kollektsiya*, 18–30.
Rak, I. V. (1997), *Avesta in Russian Translations,* St Petersburg.
Rāzī, Najm al-Dīn (2003), *The Path of God's Bondsmen from Origin to Return,* translated by H. Algar, New Haledon.
Renard, J. (1996), *Seven Doors to Islam. Spirituality and the Religious Life of Muslims*, Berkeley-Los Angeles-London.
Rudakī (2007), *Divon*, Dushanbe.
Russell, J. (1988), "Two Armenian Toponyms," *Annual of Armenian Linguistics,* 9: 47–53.
Sa'di (n.d.), *Kolliyat*, edited by M. 'Ali Forughi, Tehran.
Schwartz, M. (2012), "Transformations of the Indo-Iranian Snake-man: Myth, Language, Ethnoarcheology, and Iranian Identity," *Iranian Studies,* 275–279.
Smith, M. (2004), "Ancient Law Codes," in *Encyclopaedia of Rape*, edited by M. D. Smith, Westport-London.
Starikov, A. A. (1993), "Firdawsī and His Poem" (Firdawsī i ego poema), in *Firdawsī, Shahname*, 1, edited by C. Banu-Lahuti, A. Lahuti, A. A. Starikov, Moscow, 459–592.
Stowasser, B. F. (1994), *Women in the Qor'an, Traditions, and Interpretation*, New York-Oxford.
Ṭabarī, Muhammad b. Jarīr (1969), *al-Bayān 'an ta'wīl ay al-Qur'ān*, edited by Mahmūd Shākir and Ahmad Shākir, Cairo.
Tagirdjanov, A. T. (1948), "Notes on the Poem of Ferdousi, Yusof and Zuleykha," *Sovetskoe vostokovedenie* 5: 330–342.
al-Tha'labī, Abu ʾIshāq ʾAhmad b. Muhammad b. Ibrāhīm (1960), *Kitāb Qiṣaṣ al-anbiyā' al-musamma bi'l-Arā'is*, vol. I, Cairo.
al-Tha'labī, Abū Isḥāq Aḥmad ibn Muḥammad b. Ibrāhīm (2002), *'Arā's al-majālis fī qiṣāṣ al-anbiyā', Lives of the prophets as recounted,* translated and annotated by W. M. Brinner. Leiden-Boston.
Tolstov, S. P. (1948), *Drevniy Khorezm*, Moscow.
Ṭūsī, Nasīr al-Dīn (1978), *Akhlāq-i Nasīrī*, edited by M. Minuvī and 'Alīrizā Haydarī, Tehrān.
Vevaina, Y. S. D. (2010), "Hubris and Himmelfahrt: The Narrative Logic of Kay Us' Ascent to Heaven in Pahlavi Literature," in *Ancient and Middle Iranian Studies.* Proceedings of the 6th Conference of Iranian Studies,

held in Vienna, 18–22 September 2007, edited by M. Macuch, D. Weber and D. Durkin-Meisterernst, *Iranica* 19: 231–243.

Xenophon (1957), *The Ephesian Story by Xenophon of Ephesus*, translated from the Greek by P. Turner, illustrated by E. Fraser, London.

Yohannan, J. D. (1968), *Joseph and Potiphar's Wife in World Literature. An Anthology of the Story of the Chaste Youth and the Lustful Stepmother*, translated by various hands and edited with commentary, New York, 1968.

Yûsuf and Zalîkhâ (1970), *The Biblical Legend of Joseph and Potiphar's Wife in the Persian Version Ascribed to Abul Mansur Quasi, called Firdausi, ca. 832–1021 A.D.* Edited by H. Ethé, Amsterdam.

The Story of Furūd in the *Shāhnāma* and Elsewhere and the Apportionment of Blame

Charles Melville
University of Cambridge

Firdawsī's Story of Furūd

The story of Furūd occurs early in the reign of Kay Khusraw, newly brought to Iran by Gīv son of Gūdarz and crowned as shah in place of—or perhaps alongside—Kay Kāvūs.[1] Like Kay Khusraw, Furūd was the son of Siyāvush, but from a different wife, Jarīra, the daughter of the Tūrānian nobleman Pīrān-i Vīsa. The two young men had been brought up together. Furūd remained in Tūrān after the murder of Siyāvush, and was living quietly with his mother.[2]

On coming to the throne, Kay Khusraw quickly mounted an expedition to Tūrān, seeking revenge for the death of his father. He gave command of the army to Ṭūs even though Ṭūs had been vocal in opposing Kay Khusraw's accession to the throne, pressing his own claims and those of Farīburz, son of Kay Kāvūs. Although instructed by Kay Khusraw to enter Tūrān by a desert route to avoid disturbing the shah's half-brother, Furūd, Ṭūs disobeyed these orders and belligerently tried to eliminate Furūd when he saw the young man watching the Persian army from the high ground of his castle. Despite being told that it was Furūd, the brother of the king, Ṭūs persisted in his aggression, with the result that after a series of combats, Furūd's castle was stormed and both he and his mother, Jarīra, perished in the event. After showing some signs of remorse, Ṭūs gave Furūd an appropriate burial and moved on to the actual purpose of his expedition, which, however, also turned into a disaster for Iran.

1. As noted by Davis 1992, 47–48, the situation is ambiguous.

2. The story has been reproduced in mixed verse and prose versions, retold in prose, abridged, and edited with commentaries. See for example, Rastgār Fasā'ī 2006, 26–53; Ṭālibī 2007, 405–418; Kazzāzī 2001, 26–77, 303–452, and notes 3 and 5 below. See also the creative retelling of the story by Ātūsā Ṣāliḥi 2002, who brings out rather well Furūd's ennui and frustration at his quiet and sheltered life: he is longing for action.

So much for the outline of the story, which is relatively brief.[3] The first question to arise concerns the precise contours of the episode. For Jules Mohl, it is presented simply as one section of the reign of Kay Khusraw, preceded by his coronation, a review of the army and the dispatch of Rustam with his forces to India. For Djalal Khaleghi-Motlagh, it is a discrete episode, starting with the opening lines of Firdawsī's preamble [KM verse 1 = Mohl verse 387]:

جهانجوی چون شد سر افراز و گرد

A would-be world conqueror, if noble and heroic...

This beginning, however, is much less clearly marked in many *Shāhnāma* manuscripts, and is often introduced by a variety of headings apart from the rather infrequently found *Dāstān-i Furūd-i Siyāvush*.[4] As noted by Kumiko Yamamoto, the story stands at the head of the narrative structure of Kay Khusraw's war of revenge against Afrāsiyāb, culminating in Afrāsiyāb's defeat and the execution of Garsīvaz, responsible for Siyāvush's death, a narrative punctuated by a number of digressions.[5] Mahmoud Omidsalar sees the episode in the context of Kay Khusraw's succession to the throne, serving to eliminate his only serious rival and to restore the unity of the Iranian nobility.[6]

In the Mohl and Khaleghi-Motlagh editions, the episode does not end with Furūd's death, but continues until the return of the Iranian army in disarray after suffering a series of defeats. It therefore embraces the consequences of Ṭūs's insubordination and the similarly unsuccessful efforts of Farīburz, his replacement as military commander—an appointment one might imagine was similarly flawed. The division of the text in the printed editions closes with the verse, "Here ends the story of Furūd; now the battle with Kāmūs must be told" [M, 1700; KM, 1235], thus clearly revealing the poet's intention. Here, however, we concentrate on the start of the story with Ṭūs's command of the army and ending with the death of Furūd [M, 954; KM, 523].[7]

3. Up to the death of Furūd and Jarīra, 567 verses in the edition of Mohl (hereafter M) 1995, 582–607; 523 verses in Khaleghi-Motlagh (hereafter KM) 1992, 27–60. The story was published separately by Muḥammad Rawshan 1975. See also the convenient edition by Azizollah-e-Jowaini 2009, 77–165, with substantial notes and a prose retelling also.

4. Melville 2013.

5. Yamamoto 2003, 81–84.

6. Omidsalar 2012, 146–148. This may indeed be the result of the episode (although the reunification of the fractured nobility took some time), and Firdawsī's unstated purpose in the overall scheme; it certainly tidies up a loose end in the story of Siyāvush in Tūrān. We are more concerned here with the way the story is narrated.

7. As in the text provided by Manṣūr Rastgār 1978.

One of the most interesting elements of the episode is the way the causes of the tragedy and the shifts of blame play out through the narrative.[8] The poet's prologue gives us the essential moral of the tale:

> When a great warrior embarks on war, he should not trust his army to an enemy... someone from a noble family who cannot achieve any kind of greatness is made savage by his failure... If the heavens deny him his desires, his loyalty to the king is always suspect; ... ambition always gnaws at his heart. When you hear this tale through, you will know the nature of such a man.[9]

The frustrated noble is of course Ṭūs, disappointed in his recent bid for the throne, and it is clear that for much of the narrative it is the rash and violent Ṭūs who is blamed for what happens. Nevertheless, the poet also makes it clear that Kay Khusraw was unwise to appoint Ṭūs to command the army. Although Khusraw is depicted uniformly as a positive force, ultimately the blame for the disaster can be attributed to him; lack of wisdom (*khirad*) is a cardinal fault in Firdawsī's scheme of things.

Indeed, it seems a remarkable error of judgement to give the army to Ṭūs, and furthermore to provide him with a perfect way of compensating for his disappointment over the succession: he can harm Khusraw by harming his brother Furūd. Being told expressly to steer clear of Furūd could only be seen as provocative and at the same time as suggesting a way to hit back at Khusraw where it hurts. It is the king's error, then, that initiates the tragedy. If an explanation is sought, it could be that Khusraw hoped to win Ṭūs over by entrusting him with such an important mission and one so close to his heart; alternatively, Khusraw could have thought to get the troublesome Ṭūs out of the way and far from court, in time-honored fashion.

Having been warned by the poet's preamble to expect trouble, it is no surprise that hints of the impending drama continue. For a start, when told to avoid the route through Furūd's territory, Khusraw describes his half-brother as "a man of war, a hero and a knight, with a lofty lineage and the body of a champion; one should pass by the desert route, it is not a good idea to cross the path of lions" [KM, 40–41]. Furūd's warlike qualities are thus immediately anticipated. When Ṭūs approaches the division in the road between the desert route and the shorter one that passes through Furūd's territory, he seems to have no hesitation in disobeying Khusraw's orders, although he may have felt some pressure from the army, who clearly preferred the easier way. When he got to the front of the column, he spoke with

8. See also Djalal Khaleghi-Motlagh, "Forūd," in: *EIr* X: 107.
9. Davis 2007, 281.

the headstrong (*sar-kishān*) troops in a soothing (*narm*) voice. No one raised any objections, or pointed out that their orders were otherwise.[10]

For his part, Furūd's first reaction on seeing the approaching army was alarm, and he cleared the hillside of his grazing flocks. He is described as "inexperienced" (*nā-kār-dīda*)—hardly how Khusraw had described him—and his inclination is defensive rather than belligerent. His mother, Jarīra, however, addresses him as "warlike" (*razm-sāz*) but suggests that he offer to join the forces marching to avenge Siyāvush, after first entertaining them royally. If he had actually been able to follow Jarīra's recommendation and march at the head of the Persian troops, it can be imagined that this would have constituted a further threat to Ṭūs's authority and antagonized the Iranian commander even more: possibly a consideration in explaining his bellicose behavior.

As the story unfolds, we become aware of the intricacies and seeming inconsistencies of Firdawsī's narrative, noting the epithets with which both Furūd and Tukhvār, his advisor, are characterized, and how the blame seems to shift from Ṭūs and onto them, until the unfortunate dénouement.

Thus Tukhvār is bold (*dilāvar*); a preserver of tradition (*sarāyanda* 'singer');[11] thoughtful (*rāy-zan*) in advising Furūd to calm down; experienced in war (*razm-dīda*); a man of vision (*mard-i bīnā*).[12] When he advises Furūd to shoot Rīvnīz's horse rather than the man, he is experienced (*kār-dīda*) [KM, 260]; when he—perhaps belatedly—advises Furūd to retreat to the castle and avoid conflict with Ṭūs, he is again a "singer" (*sarāyanda*) [KM, 288]. The positive epithets continue until Tukhvār again advises retreat, but then comes an interesting verse:

سخن هر چه از پیش بایست گفت   نگفت و همی داشت اندر نهفت

he said what he should have said before; (but) he didn't say it (before) and kept it hidden [KM, 300].

10. As noted in KM's critical apparatus, p. 31, al-Bundarī's translation states that Gūdarz concurred with the decision, cf. the Persian translation by Ayati 2003, 174. Older editions include a passage given to Gūdarz's effort to remind Ṭūs, in vain, of the king's instructions, e.g., M, 448–450; cf. KM, p. 30, n. 27, and the retelling of Ṭālibī 2007, 406.

11. For a discussion of this term, see Davidson 2013b, 20–29. Davidson does not refer to these instances of the use of the term, which are difficult to accommodate into her theory of the "singer" as a performer of oral poetry, this being entirely irrelevant to the context in which Tukhvār and Furūd find themselves. At best, we might agree to equate it with the term *dihqān*, representative of the old social elite, and a repository therefore of traditional knowledge, which in theory at least he should have been able to pass on to Furūd as a wise counselor; cf. examples 14a and 14b in Davidson 2013b, 27.

12. KM, 103, 110, 153, 251, 257.

That is, the poet now blames Tukhvār for not having counseled Furūd to retreat to the castle from the very beginning, and this indeed was Bahrām's advice when they first met, if Bahrām did not return himself to Furūd [KM, 218–20]. Immediately, Tukhvār is described as "an ignorant and worthless advisor" (بی مایه دستور ناکار دان) [KM, 301]. Thereafter, Tukhvār's role declines and he is barely mentioned again except as Furūd's interlocutor.

Meanwhile, Furūd's own stock has followed a similar downward trajectory. He starts as a young man (*javān*) and a hero (*nāmvar*); he deals with Bahrām proudly but sensibly when they first meet. But his first reaction on seeing Rīvnīz coming up the mountain instead of Bahrām is to reach for his bow and arrow, and he is routinely described by Firdawsī as a warlike king (*shāh-i jangī*) and a raging lion or lion-man (*shīr-i zhiyān, mard-i shīr*) thereafter. He is increasingly incensed by Tukhvār's accounts of the prowess of his attackers, which instead of provoking caution, merely inflames him to prove himself superior. He becomes angry (*tīz shud*) when Tukhvār finally urges him to retreat to the castle [KM, 292], and the immature decision instead to shoot Ṭūs's horse—influenced now also by the cheers of the girls watching from the battlements of the castle—again marks the turning point. The crucial lines here are expressed by Gīv, after Ṭūs has come back down the mountain on foot, the taunts of the girls echoing in his ears:[13]

چنین گفت کاین را خود اندازه نیست   رخ نامداران بدین تازه نیست
اگر شهریارست با گوشوار   چه گیرد چنین لشکر گشن خوار
اگر طوس یکبار تیزی نمود   زمانه پر آزار گشت از فرود
گر او پور جم است و مغز قباد   یکی در بنادانی اندر گشاد

He said, "this is beyond the limit, the heroes' cheeks grow haggard
Even if he is a prince with (royal) ear-rings, how can he hold such a mighty army in contempt? ...
Even if Ṭūs did once act rashly, the world has become full of strife through Furūd ...
Even if he be the son of Jamshīd or the essence of Qubād, he has opened a door (to disaster) in his ignorance."

When Gīv then comes up the mountain against Furūd, the latter has the same premonitions of disaster and the collapse of Kay Khusraw's enterprise against Afrāsiyāb, but Furūd's "ignorance" is now compounded by Tukhvār's lack of knowledge (*bī-dānishī*), sowing thorns in the meadow—the thorns being his provocative words of praise for Gīv [KM, 340].

As the final inevitable climax nears, due to Bīzhan's warlike determi-

13. KM, 323–324, 326, 330.

nation and courage, Furūd once more becomes a young king (*shāh-i javān*) and even Tukhvār, in giving his last (and persistent) advice to shoot only Bīzhan's horse, is once more a *sarāyanda* [KM, 394, 396]. As Furūd retreats to the castle in the face of Bīzhan's onslaught, he is the "precious" (*girānmāya*) Furūd [KM, 412]. In the final encounters, all his princely, warlike, and heroic attributes are restored: he is young, a lion-man, a brave man, a warlike lion, etc. [KM, 457–61].

Furūd himself, on his deathbed, recognizes Bīzhan as his nemesis, "for it is he who has taken my pure soul, he is my Doom in my days of youth" [KM, 472], even though the fatal blow was actually struck by Ruhhām. And, in seeking responsibility for the tragedy, Bīzhan also must take his share of blame—not only because he broke the pattern of the previous encounters, and refused to retreat when his horse was shot from under him, but also because of his raging disrespect for his father, Gīv, and the rashness with which he is repeatedly characterized by the poet from his first appearance in the story: *Bīzhan-i tīz mard* [KM, 356]. Thus first Gīv tells him, "you have no brain, no sense and no wisdom" [KM, 364]; then Gustaham, whom he approaches in order to borrow a good horse, tells him that "this is not the way, wisdom knows nothing of this rashness" [KM, 382]. Finally, Bahrām also accuses Bīzhan for his hotheadedness: "From Ruhhām and the hothead Bīzhan, nothing good comes to the world" [KM, 499]. Despite his bravery and fighting qualities, the negative characteristics attributed to Bīzhan make clear his own share of responsibility for the disaster.[14]

It is also the case, however, that Fate has already determined the outcome:

سر بخـت مـرد جـوان گشته بود

The young man's Fate had changed [KM, 451].

Echoing the familiar sentiment, typical of Firdawsī, expressed right from the outset.

The fortune of the young man was clouded with dust;
when the firmament turns crookedly from its zenith,
neither love nor rage are of any use [KM, 108–9].

This pre-ordained outcome is also foreshadowed in the dream of Furūd's mother, Jarīra, the night before the fatal battle.[15] But Firdawsī, equally char-

14. For a sympathetic account of Bīzhan's character and his role in the story of Furūd, see Vāmeqi 2001, 29–38.

15. Possibly also in her anxiety when the first news of the approaching Iranian army reaches her, as articulated in some retellings of the story, cf. Ṭālibī 2007, 407, and especially

acteristically, is not content to leave the blame for the tragedy with the random workings of Fate: the agency by which the result is achieved is the clash of wills and senseless belligerence of those on both sides, whose warrior code makes them more like each other than distinct; and both are hell-bent on conflict. Bīzhan's report on Furūd's prowess, which in view of what had happened on their first encounter must be taken as sarcastic, has the effect of inflaming Ṭūs to vengeance against the "malignant Turk" (*Turk-i bad-khvāh*) [KM, 425].

By the end, the blame comes back firmly onto Ṭūs, who is reprimanded by Gūdarz, Gīv, and Bahrām. It is his hastiness, rashness, and folly (*tundī, tīzī*, being *bī-khirad*), as usual, that have sent not only Furūd, but also Rīvnīz and Zarāsp to their deaths:

که تیزی نه کار سپهبد بود　　سپهبد که تندی کند بد کند

For haste is not the mark of a commander; the commander who acts rashly is evil [KM, 512].

Gīv had been party to the senseless attacks on Furūd and his accusations have the air of passing the blame elsewhere. Bahrām—the former companion of Siyāvush—however, was the initial go-between and the one who did his best to stem Ṭūs's aggression. The whole episode ends with the death of Bahrām, noble to the last. Ṭūs's punishment comes sooner, with his demotion from command of the army, and the public humiliation first before the troops and then back at the court of Kay Khusraw. The latter too is punished by the death of Furūd for his original folly in appointing Ṭūs. In his letter summoning Ṭūs to return, Khusraw writes:

> I told him, "Do not take the road to Jaram; do not breathe on Kalāt and Sipadkūh; for that way is Furūd and he has an army—one who is a warrior and has noble lineage—he does not know, at bottom, who this army is; they are an army from Iran but what are they doing? ..." [KM, 828–30].

Some manuscripts insert an extra line here, "he will certainly come fighting down the mountain, their Time will be up for a great many chiefs," [M, 1266][16] presumably to make explicit the underlying concern, that the warlike Furūd will react in the wrong way to the approach of the Iranian army. Furūd is, after all, at least half a "Turk," with a Tūrānian mother and

---

Ṣāliḥi 2002, 18–28. There is some support for this in M, 467, though more probably it is Furūd who is anxious for Jarīra rather than vice versa.

16. Supported in one very early ms., British Library Add. 12,103 (1276); cf. KM, p. 78, n. 16.

living in the "enemy" land.[17] Despite his connections with the Iranians through Siyāvush, he inhabits ambiguous territory both geographically and psychologically, though as noted above, his lion-like prowess and warrior's pride equate him with the Iranian champions who become his unwitting opponents.

It is clear, therefore, that "all are punishéd" and no one prospers after the tragedy, for which all are to blame: everyone involved—with the exception of Bahrām—is at one stage or another accused of lack of wisdom, whether it be the shah himself, Ṭūs, Tukhvār, Furūd, or Bīzhan.

Prose Accounts Before and After Firdawsī

There are many other turns of phrase and points of detail that make the story told by Firdawsī of compelling interest, including elements that echo other episodes in the epic. But if, limiting ourselves to the main topic addressed here, it is possible to discern some ambiguity in his treatment of responsibility in the story of Furūd, it is worth pausing to consider what sources might have been available to him, at least in the light of the earliest account at our disposal.[18] According to al-Ṭabarī (d. 923):

> ... they say that Ṭūs committed a fatal error: namely, when he was near the city in which Furūdh dwelled, somehow hostilities broke out between them [in the course of which] Furūdh perished.[19]

This remains quite close to the thrust of Firdawsī's version, though enormously abbreviated, and—like all the other tellings of the tale—devoid of the psychological penetration of the *Shāhnāma* and Firdawsī's concern to draw morals from the narrative.

The story is radically and remarkably different in Bal'amī's version of Ṭabarī (c. 963), where the blame is laid squarely on Furūd himself:[20]

> Then Ṭūs took the army and headed for Turkistan. When he reached Furūd's town, Furūd sent out an army. Ṭūs said, "You are the brother of my king, and Kay Khusraw has ordered me to act well in your

17. This double aspect of Furūd's nature is interestingly brought out in the retelling of the story by Ṣāliḥi 2002.

18. I do not intend here to enter the debate on Firdawsī's sources, for which see Davidson 2013a, esp. 22–41; Davis 1996, 48–57; Yamamoto 2003, esp. 1–8. The story is not mentioned at all by Abū Ḥanīfa Dīnawārī, *al-Akhbār al-ṭiwāl* or Abū Manṣūr Tha'ālibī, *Ghurar akhbār mulūk al-Furs*.

19. al-Ṭabarī 1881, 605–606, tr. Perlmann 1987, 8–9.

20. Bal'amī 1998–9, 438–439.

> district; go back, and may this kingship be yours, so that I can pass by and lead the army against Afrāsiyāb." Furūd did not obey, and did not turn back; he fought with Ṭūs and Furūd and his army were killed.

We cannot be sure of course that Firdawsī was aware of Bal'amī's version of Ṭabarī,[21] but this is a plausible source for the culpability of Furūd in the débâcle, which is hinted at several times in the course of the *Shāhnāma* text, and it matches what Khusraw evidently thought would happen if Furūd saw the seemingly hostile force approaching.

The question then shifts: if the "original" story was that Furūd brought disaster upon himself, why did Firdawsī choose instead to make him an innocent victim? A man who:

> ... died a more abject and lamentable death than his father; the killer of Siyāvush was not an attendant (*chākir*), his mother was not killed at his bedside, with his castle burned like a reed, or his family and belongings uprooted and consumed by fire [KM, 491–3].

The reason must be to emphasize the moral objectives of the narration: the initial misjudgement of Khusraw; the thwarted ambition and violent pride of Ṭūs; the anger of Furūd in response and the hot-headed aggressiveness of the Iranian warriors involved; the failure of Tukhvār to assess the situation correctly; and the outcome that shows the price to be paid all round for these human vices and failings, from the multiple casualties before Ṭūs led the army on to resume their mission, to the failure of the expedition in the war that followed.

As for later narratives, these for the most part follow the trend of the story in the *Shāhnāma*. The *Mujmal al-tawārīkh* (c. 1126), says that Furūd was killed by the rashness (*tīzkārī*) of Ṭūs-i Nawzar. Ṭūs was stripped of his command, but restored later on Rustam's intervention.[22] Ibn al-Balkhī (c. 1116) also follows the *Shāhnāma* rather closely and in relatively full detail.[23] Ḥamd-Allāh Mustawfī (c. 1330) has the story very briefly under the reign of Kay Khusraw, who ordered Ṭūs not to fight with Siyāvush's son, called Furūd, in Tūrān. Ṭūs scorned his words, and fought Furūd. Furūd was killed in that battle. Ṭūs went (on) to fight Afrāsiyāb and came back defeated to Iran.[24]

On the other hand, in the seventeenth-century *Lughat-i Shāhnāma* of 'Abd al-Qādir Baghdādī, the story is briefly explained by saying that in the

21. Or even that this is what Bal'amī said, given the state of the text as transmitted, cf. Peacock 2007.

22. Anon. 1939, 48.

23. Ibn al-Balkhī 1921, 44–45.

24. Mustawfī 1983, p. 89.

battle between Ṭūs and Furūd's castle, Furūd was killed, *but they [the Iranians] didn't know* he was the brother of Kay Khusraw.[25]

More interesting is the abridgment written for the Mughal governor in Ghazna in 1653, the *Tārīkh-i Dil-gushā-yi Shamshīrkhānī* of Tavakkul Beg.[26] There are many departures from the text of the *Shāhnāma* in this episode. Kay Khusraw divides command of the army of revenge for Siyāvush between Ṭūs and Farīburz (whereas the *Shāhnāma* names only Ṭūs), and omits the entire moral framework for the story of Furūd that follows (starting with the warning about the disloyalty of those who bear a grudge).

Ordered to leave Furūd's territory alone, Farīburz does so, but strong-willed Ṭūs takes the direct route that he prefers. Ṭūs sends his son-in-law Rīv with a message to Furūd saying that he means him no harm (thus omitting Bahrām's mission), but Furūd does not believe him; they fight, and Rīv is killed. Ṭūs's son (not named) meets the same fate and Ṭūs then attacks with the whole army. Many of the forces of Tukhvār (named as Furūd's uncle) are killed, but when Furūd sees Ṭūs among the besiegers, he sallies forth and shoots his horse. Gīv suffers the same treatment, as does Bīzhan, who asks for a brief delay before their fight is resumed. In combat, Bīzhan's spear grazes Furūd, who retreats to his fortress: he hurls down so many rocks that Bīzhan is himself wounded and retires to Ṭūs.

Ṭūs resolves to attack next day and kill all in the fortress. Furūd's mother here is called the daughter of Jarīr, one of Afrāsiyāb's champions. Her dream and Furūd's response are essentially as in the *Shāhnāma*; in the ensuing battle, he and Bīzhan are fighting when Ruhhām comes up from behind and strikes Furūd a blow on the head, from which he falls from his horse and dies.[27] This again is different from the *Shāhnāma*; his mother rushes up, cradles her son in her lap and kills herself with a dagger.

The Iranians draw a parallel between the innocent death of Furūd and that of his father Siyāvush; Bahrām (here making his first appearance) blames Ṭūs for his actions (a role given chiefly to Gūdarz in the *Shāhnāma*), and asks how he will answer to the shah. The story then moves on to the next scene.

Although this narrative is similar (at least the sequence of persons involved in the encounters) to that in the *Shāhnāma*, the details are sufficiently different for it to be hard to describe the text as an abridgment of the original, and beside the action, all discussion and comment is

25. Baghdādī 2003, 285.

26. Tavakkul Beg 2005, 223–226. A separate study of this work is in preparation.

27. In Ṭālibī's retelling of the story, Ruhhām strikes Furūd on the head with his sword, and as Furūd fights on, Bīzhan strikes him on the helmet with a club, Ṭālibī 2007, 417; cf. M, 882.

stripped away, to leave a story deprived of human drama and psychological interest. Nor is it clear why the details should have been altered, for they do not lead to a different interpretation of the story: on the whole, Furūd's behavior is again more clearly blameworthy, as he didn't wish to believe in Ṭūs's peaceful intentions (whereas Firdawsī shows that his intentions were not in fact peaceful), but the nuances of the shifting motivations are lost. The *Shamshīrkhānī* text does, nevertheless, contain rather specific traces of the narrative tradition that lays the blame on Furūd's own impetuosity and belligerence.

Finally, it is interesting to note a much earlier attempt to render the *Shāhnāma* in prose, by the thirteenth-century author al-Bundarī, whose Arabic translation, completed in 624/1227, is almost the earliest witness to the text. The work, like the later Tavakkul Beg's, is also an abridgement, so it is not necessarily a guide to what might have been added by later copyists, but it does have elements that are distinct from the current authoritative reading of the text by Khaleghi-Motlagh. One such, as noted earlier, is Gūdarz's acquiescence in Ṭūs's disobedience to the shah's orders. Otherwise, it is more a case of passages omitted, such as Bahrām's efforts to dissuade first the Iranian troops, and then Rīvnīz, from going to fight Furūd. Jarīra's dream and Furūd's deathbed speeches are also omitted.

Of more interest to the topic addressed in this paper, al-Bundarī has left out the deliberations between Furūd and Tukhvār over how to deal with Rīv (*sic*) and Zarāsp—Tukhvār's role is only mentioned when Ṭūs himself comes on the scene. Furthermore, Gīv's speech noted above, remarking that Furūd had gone too far and was now at fault himself, is left out, and the fairly lengthy passage of blame leveled at Ṭūs at the end, when the Iranian heroes find Furūd and Jarīra lying dead together, is very greatly reduced.[28] In other words, as in most other treatments of the story, the motif of responsibility and the twists of culpability that flow back and forth in Firdawsī's masterful narrative are entirely missing; the details of the story are related, but without their inner tension. Even the opening preamble, concerning the stupidity of appointing a commander hostile to the king, is absent.

Conclusion

In conclusion, although the story of Furūd is relatively well known and its interest has already been noted, this article has attempted to look at the

28. al-Bundarī 1932, tr. Āyatī 2003, 176, 177, 178.

text in more detail to see how Firdawsī achieves the compelling narrative we have, so much richer than the bald rehearsals in the few prose texts that include this episode, and how the element of Furūd's aggression and inexperience, leading to a frustrated desire to prove himself, also influence the outcome.

Bibliography

Anon. (1939), *Mujmal al-tawārīkh wa'l-qiṣaṣ*, ed. Muḥammad Taqī Bahār, Tehran.

Baghdādī, 'Abd al-Qādir (2003), *Lughat-i Shāhnāma*, ed. Karl G. Salemann, trans. T. H. Sobhani and Alî Rāvaghī, Tehran.

Bal'amī, Abū 'Alī (1998–9), *Tārīkhnāma-yi Ṭabarī*, ed. M. Rawshan, 5 vols., Tehran.

al-Bundarī, Fatḥ b. 'Alī al-Iṣfahānī (1932), *al-Shāhnāmah*, ed. 'A. 'Aẓẓam, Cairo; tr. 'Abd al-Muḥammad Āyatī (2003), *Shāhnāma-yi Firdawsī taḥrīr-i 'arabī*, Tehran.

Davidson, Olga M. (2013a), *Poet and Hero in the Persian Book of Kings*, third edition, Boston.

—— (2013b), *Comparative Literature and Classical Persian Poetics. Seven Essays*, second edition, Boston.

Davis, Dick (1992), *Epic and Sedition. The Case of Ferdowsi's Shāhnāmeh*, Fayetteville.

—— (1996), "The Problem of Ferdowsî's Sources," *Journal of the American Oriental Society* 116 no. 1: 48–57.

Firdawsī, Abu'l-Qāsim (1842), *Shāhnāma*, ed. and tr. Jules Mohl, *Le Livre des Rois*, vol. II, Paris; Persian text only (1995), ed. Jahāngīr Afkārī, vol. II, Tehran.

Firdawsī, Abu'l-Qāsim (1992), *Shāhnāma*, ed. Djalal Khaleghi-Motlagh, *Abu'l-Qasem Ferdowsi, The Shahnameh (Book of Kings)*, vol. III, Costa Mesa and New York.

Firdawsī, Abu'l-Qāsim (2007), *Shahnameh. The Persian Book of Kings*, tr. Dick Davis, London.

Ibn al-Balkhī (1921), *Fārsnāma*, ed. G. Le Strange and R.A. Nicholson, London.

Jowaini, Azizollah (2009), *The story of Forood-e Seyawash*, Tehran.

Kazzāzī, Mīr Jalāl al-Dīn (1994), *Nāma-yi Bāstān. Virāyish va Guzārish-i Shāhnāma-yi Firdawsī*, vol. IV, Tehran.

Khaleghi-Motlagh, Djalal (1999), "Forūd," in: *EIr* X, 107.

Melville, Charles (2013), "Rubrics and Chapter Headings in Texts of the Shahnameh," *Nāmeh-ye Bahārestān* 20 [in press].

Mustawfī, Ḥamd-Allāh (1983), *Tārīkh-i Guzīda*, ed. 'A. Navā'ī, Tehran.

Omidsalar, M. (2012), *Iran's Epic and America's Empire. A Handbook for a Generation in Limbo*, Santa Monica.

Peacock, A. C. S. (2007), *Medieval Islamic Historiography and Political Legitimacy. Bal'amī's Tārīkhnāma*, Abingdon and New York.

Rastgār, Manṣūr (1978), *Bar-guzīda-yi Dāstān-i Furūd-i Siyāvush*, 2nd printing, Tehran (abridgment).
Rastgār Fasā'ī, M. (2006), ed. *Pādshāhī-yi Kaykhusraw, Qiṣṣa-hā-yi Shāhnāma*, vol. III, Tehran (abridgment), pp. 26–42.
Rawshan, Muḥammad (1975), *Dāstān-i Furūd az Shāhnāma-yi Firdawsī*, Tehran.
Ṣāliḥī, Ātūsā (2002), *Qiṣṣa-hā-yi Shāhnāma. Furūd va Jarīra*, Tehran.
al-Ṭabarī, Muḥammad b. Jarīr (1881–2), *Ta'rīkh al-rusul wa'l-mulūk*, ed. M. J. de Goeje, vol. I, Leiden; tr. Moshe Perlmann (1987), *The History of al-Tabarī, vol. IV. The Ancient Kingdoms*, Albany.
Ṭālibī, Fulūr (2007), *Dāstān-hā-yi asātirī-yi Shāhnāma*, Mashhad.
Tavakkul Beg (2005), *Tārīkh-i Dil-gushā-yi Shamshīrkhānī*, ed. Tahira Parveen Akram, Islamabad.
Vāmeqi, Iraj (2001), *Bizhan-nāme. On Shāhnāme*, Tehran.
Yamamoto, Kumiko (2003), *The Oral Background of Persian Epics. Storytelling and Poetry*, Leiden.

Shāhnāma Images and *Shāhnāma* Settings in Medieval Iran

Marianna Shreve Simpson
Philadelphia, Pennsylvania

Since the mid-twentieth century, if not earlier, much scholarly ink has been spilled over the chronology of, and specifically the starting date for, the tradition of illustrating Ferdowsi's *Shāhnāma* in manuscript form. The problem gained fresh currency during the poem's 2010 millennial year and was addressed repeatedly in numerous publications, exhibitions, and symposia related to the epic commemorations.[1] While the issue is likely to remain an ongoing subject of scholarly concern and discussion, it is commonly accepted that narrative images related to stories in the Persian Book of Kings were being produced several centuries before Ferdowsi set to work on his great epic poem and that this artistic engagement with epic kings and heroes continued—and seemingly with greater frequency—during later medieval times.[2] The aim of the present essay is to consider the place and role, the impact and influence of Ferdowsi's epic poem in and on the visual arts of Iran during these times, that is, roughly the twelfth and thirteenth centuries, and to take a fresh look at *Shāhnāma* images, both textual and representational, on medieval objects and in buildings, with the goal of assessing both the cultural context and purpose of such imagery.

The current assessment begins with a fragmentary ceramic star tile (Figure 1), comprising three and one-half of its original eight points and with an inscribed band in its upper section that identifies its decoration as relating to a *Shāhnāma* episode involving the hero Furūd (Museum of Fine Arts, Boston).[3] Although the tile's dimensions have long been recorded in

1. Simpson 2004, 9–25; Simpson 2009–12, with an extensive bibliography and a listing of millennium exhibitions and conferences, 2010–11.

2. Simpson 1985. Both here and elsewhere, I argue that images associated today with Ferdowsi's *Shāhnāma* did not necessarily originate in Ferdowsi's *Shāhnāma*, but may have been inspired by oral versions of tales that Ferdowsi incorporated into his epic text. For the sake of convenience, however, the term "*Shāhnāma* images" is used in the present essay with reference to representations that could have derived either from oral or written narrative sources.

3. Gemeente Museum 1927, cat. no. 161; Hall 1934, fig. 14; Pope and Ackerman 1938–39, 5: pl. 706; Pope and Ackerman 1945, pl. 86; Pinder-Wilson 1957, pl. 22; Sims 2002, 93, no. 3.

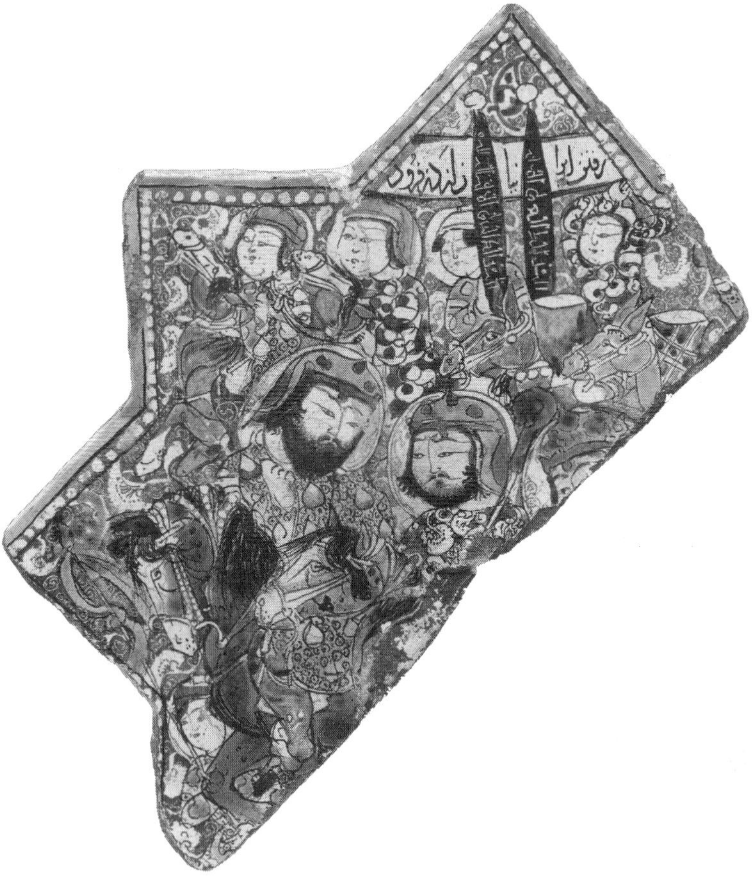

Figure 1. Fragmentary Star Tile, early 13th century, ceramic over-glaze painted with enamel and luster. Courtesy Museum of Fine Arts Boston, 31.495. Photograph © 2013 Museum of Fine Arts.

its current fragmentary state (9–1/2 inches at its highest point and 6–1/4 at its widest), its original size would have been quite a bit larger, and measured about 11–1/2 inches in both height and width.[4] In and of themselves, these

4. These dimensions have been arrived at by rudimentary projection and reconstruction, and by comparison with other intact star tiles of roughly the same period. See: Arık and Arık 2008, 197; Watson 1985, 123 and figs. 106–108; Carboni and Masuya, Tomoko 1993, cat. no. 7. The star tile was already in fragmentary condition when it entered the Museum of Fine Art's collection in 1931. Its impressive size and overall visual impact were very effectively demonstrated during the 2010 exhibition, *Heroic Gestes: Epic Tales from Firdawsi's Shahnama*, at

dimensions are meaningless, however, because such a tile is unlikely to have been made as a singleton, that is, as an individual artistic production.[5] Rather it would have belonged to a set of star tiles alternating with cruciform tiles and forming an ensemble that would have covered the interior wall or walls of a building. While no such expanse of star and cross tiles from late twelfth- or early thirteenth-century Iran has survived in situ today, it is easy to imagine, on the basis of contemporary fragments found in Anatolia, as well as somewhat later Persian panels, that the architectural setting for and installation of Boston's fragmentary star tile would have been quite grand.[6] This assumption can be supported on the basis of the tile's presumed original size and arrangement, and especially on the basis of its decor, which combines the two ceramic techniques of *mīnā'ī* and luster. The first was used for the tile's figural imagery and involved painting the design with bright colors, of which some were applied prior to a first glaze firing and others as enamels over the glaze in a subsequent firing and at a different temperature. The second technique of luster was used for the tile's foliate background and involved over-glaze painting with a pigment containing silver or copper compounds, and firing the piece yet again in a reduction kiln, leaving a metallic sheen on the surface.[7] So technically speaking, the manufacture of the tile and its presumed mates was very labor-intensive, which is doubtless why very few Persian ceramics seem to have been decorated in this particular combination. Furthermore the quality of its decoration, both in terms of design and execution, is extremely high.[8] In short, the fragmentary Boston star tile is indeed, as acclaimed in its label for a 2010 *Shāhnāma* exhibition at Harvard University, a veritable "tour de force of the ceramic arts."

Being both labor-intensive in its production and high-quality in its decoration, the tile would have been extremely expensive, which is another reason for supposing that it originally formed part of the wall covering or revetment in a palatial or aristocratic or otherwise wealthy setting. Even without any existing examples of contemporary interiors, the evidence gleaned from medieval Persian literary texts makes it all but certain that

---

the Arthur M. Sackler Museum, Harvard University, where the tile hung next to several manuscript illustrations.

5. But on this point see Watson 1985, 130.

6. For contemporary Anatolian star and cruciform tiles fragments and reconstructed panels, see: Roxburgh 2005, cat. no. 68; Arık and Arık 2008, 197–203 and ills. 9–11 and 234, figs. 169–170; for later Persian panels, see Watson 1985, pl. K; O'Kane 2009, fig. 2.18. For comments about the architectural setting of such tiles, see: Sims 2002, 93; Masuya 2002, 102.

7. Koss, McCarthy, et al. 2009; Watson 1985, 31–36.

8. I am grateful to Blythe McCarthy, senior scientist, Freer and Sackler Galleries, Smithsonian Institution, Washington, D.C., for her views on the tile's technique and quality.

Shāhnāma verses, and probably also *Shāhnāma* images, adorned the inside of Persian palaces, particularly throne and banqueting halls, during the twelfth and early thirteenth centuries and perhaps even as early as the eleventh.[9] There is also the evidence of wall painting, such as the rare fresco fragment depicting two registers of *Shāhnāma* scenes (Harvard Art Museums), of which the lower one is particularly relevant for the present discussion.[10]

Of perhaps even greater value for visualizing the star tile's original context are the decorative elements identified as coming from the palace complex of Takht-i Solaymān, built as a summer residence in northwestern Iran by the Il-Khanid Mongol ruler Abaqa in the 1270s and generally regarded as conforming to Persian traditions of palace decoration developed well before Takht-i Solaymān's construction.[11] Although the site today is in ruins, archaeological excavations and art historical investigations have reconstructed parts of its original interior decoration, which included ceramic wall coverings in various techniques and designs. Among these are frieze tiles decorated with verses and images from the *Shāhnāma*.[12] The tiles with *Shāhnāma* verses share the same size and layout, so it may be assumed that they belonged to the same frieze, although there is no certainty as to how and where they would have been installed at Takht-i Solaymān.[13] The figural tiles, on the other hand, vary somewhat in their dimensions and de-

9. Melikian-Chirvani 1984, 1988, 1991, 1996, 1997; O'Kane 2009, 36. See also Masuya 2002, 102.

10. Pope and Ackerman 1938–39, 5: pl. 554; Adamova 2008, 2, fig. 1. While Adamova's identification of the upper scene as Sindokht reproaching her daughter Rūdāba may be problematic, the lower register clearly represents the *Shāhnāma* king Feridun mounted on Barmāya, the cow that nurtured him as a child, and leading the captured tyrant Zahhāk, the snakes wriggling over his head, to Mt. Damāvand. The figure in front is the blacksmith Kāva, who assisted Feridun in his overthrow of Zahhāk and his reclaiming the Iranian throne. This image actually does not correspond to the Feridun and Zahhāk story as recounted by Ferdowsi in his *Shāhnāma*; rather it seems to be composed of various independent, portrait-like units, each of which may be identified by certain distinctive and specific attributes that are sufficient to recall heroic action and that together form a group scene symbolizing an entire narrative sequence nowadays familiar from Ferdowsi's poem, but perhaps even more familiar to medieval artists from other, *oral* versions of the Feridun and Zahhāk tale. For a fuller exposition of this point, see Simpson 1985.

11. Masuya 2002.

12. Masuya 2002, 91–103.

13. Gyuzalian 1949, 1951, 1952. See also Melekian-Chirvani 1984, 1988, 1991, 1996, 1997, as well as Masuya 2002, and O'Kane 2009, 48–50. These inscribed frieze tiles may have been set above panels of smaller tiles, as suggested in Komaroff and Carboni 2002, cat. no. 82; Masuya 2002, 96 suggests that they were placed higher up than the walls' dado tiling, which reached to a height of about six feet. For *Shāhnāma* inscriptions in other fourteenth-century buildings, including a mosque, see Watson 1975, 65–67; Watson 1985, 155; O'Kane 2009, 51. For general comments based on the evidence of Anatolian tiles, see Arık and Arık 2008, 198–199.

signs and so must have come from different ensembles and probably from different rooms or at least different walls within Takht-i Solaymān. All this confirms the extent to which *Shāhnāma* stories dominated the interiors of this particular palace of the 1270s, and possibly also the interiors of earlier thirteenth- and even twelfth-century palatial buildings such as the one for which the fragmentary star tile in Boston may be presumed to have been made.

There is more to be said about this tile's installation and setting, but let us now turn to its iconography. Even in its fragmentary state, it is possible to make out that the center depicts two large and bearded horsemen, with one holding an animal-headed mace, and the head of a third man. Above these figures are two smaller riders, a bearer with two furled flags, a drummer on horseback and part of a second drummer to the right. The broken remnant of the tile's lower half contains yet another figure, who seems to be on foot and holding a long pole, or possibly a spear, adorned at the top with banners. Such a figural composition could depict various events, including a ceremonial parade or a pilgrim caravan, as illustrated, for instance, in the *Maqāmāt* manuscript of 1237,[14] although the mace and the helmet-like headgear of the tile's central figures suggest a military scene.

As for the tile's specific subject, this is clarified by the inscription, the equivalent of a picture caption or rubric, in the upper point, which reads: *Raftan-i Īrānīan az dez-i Forud* ("the Iranians leaving Furūd's fortress"). Although this is not a *Shāhnāma* verse, it does refer to a *Shāhnāma* episode, which occurs at the very start of the reign of the legendary Kayanian king Kay Khusraw.[15] This virtuous *Shāhnāma* monarch had vowed to avenge the death of his father, prince Siyāvush, who was murdered before Kay Khusraw's birth in the enemy kingdom of Tūrān. The background to this murder is complicated: Siyāvush was the legitimate heir to the Iranian throne until he had a falling out with his father, the shah Kay Kāvūs. The Iranian prince then took refuge in Tūrān, where he had two consorts and fathered two sons; one was Kay Khusraw, who as a youth fled to Iran and succeeded his grandfather on the Iranian throne. Siyāvush's other son was named Furūd and he lived in a mountainous region of Tūrān called Kalāt. Kay Khusraw begins his revenge against Tūrān by sending out an expeditionary force of Iranian troops with strict orders to avoid the region governed by his half-brother Furūd. Once on the march, the army's headstrong commanding general, Ṭūs, immediately disobeys his shah's orders and heads right for Kalāt and

14. Ettinghausen 1977, 118–119.

15. Khaleghi-Motlagh 1992, 3: 27–102; Davis 2000, 2: 91–120. See also Charles Melville's contribution to the present volume.

Furūd's mountaintop castle. There then ensues a series of one-on-one fights in which Furūd kills two of Ṭūs's men and shoots Ṭūs's horse out from under him, before being ambushed by a pair of Iranian warriors and mortally wounded. Fleeing back into his fortress, Furūd soon dies, whereupon his mother and womenfolk all kill themselves to avoid the expected Iranian ravage and plunder. Ṭūs and his troops do storm the castle, but when they see Furūd, a son of noble Siyāvush and brother of their reigning monarch Kay Khusraw, lying dead with his mother beside him, their war cries turn to "bloody tears."[16] So instead of razing the mountaintop castle, they build a tomb there for Furūd and the fallen Iranian warriors, which they then seal up before sorrowfully continuing on with their military campaign.

This précis of the Furūd story would seem to clarify that the Boston star tile represents the Iranians' departure from Kalāt, and specifically from the tomb where they have buried Furūd and two of their own men.[17] It might not even be too much of a stretch to identify the figure holding the blue mace as the Iranian warrior Bahrām, whom Furūd met before the start of the conflict and to whom he gave his own mace, encrusted with turquoise.[18] Although this scene is the story's denouement, it is not exactly the climactic or most dramatic moment,[19] and certainly would not even be recognizable as part of the Furūd tale without the identifying inscription, precisely because the group looks like such a generic military entourage. Indeed, the very presence of this inscription suggests that the tile's imagery needed identification even at the time it was made.[20]

Be that as it may, it seems safe to conclude, as already proposed, that the star tile was part of an extensive architectural ensemble[21] and that it depicts the ending of a tale, presumably Ferdowsi's version, about Furūd. Taking all this one step further, we may surmise that the tile formed the last element

16. Davis 2000, 2: 119.

17. Simpson 1979, 225–226.

18. Simpson 1979, 104.

19. Brend and Melville 2010, 32. As a whole, however, the Furūd story is considered one of the *Shāhnāma*'s most dramatic. See Khaleghi-Motlagh 2001, X:107; Blair and Bloom 2006, 68.

20. Simpson 1979, 226; Sims 2002, 93. Interestingly, this inscription is identical in its syntax to the rubrics in *Shāhnāma* manuscripts of the Mongol period. Sometimes called chapter headings, these rubrics are actually descriptors of ongoing narrative action and appear at periodic and seemingly random intervals throughout early epic volumes. Scholarly advocates for the existence of illustrated *Shāhnāma* manuscripts in pre-Mongol times doubtless would regard the Boston tile inscription as reflecting lost book practice. Conversely, I propose here that the manuscript rubrics reflect the continuation of a practice developed for objects, and specifically for twelfth- and early thirteenth-century architectural decoration where there is otherwise no written text to serve as a clue to the epic imagery. Admittedly, the origin and function of *Shāhnāma* rubrics requires further research, comparable to O'Kane 2007.

21. Brend and Melville 2010, 32.

of a much larger narrative display, with previous star tiles in the sequence representing the story's beginning and key moments that followed, such as Kay Khusraw reviewing his troops, Kay Khusraw appointing Ṭūs to lead the expedition, Furūd meeting Bahrām, Furūd shooting Ṭūs's horse out from under him, a wounded Furūd retreating to his castle, Furūd's death, and the Iranians mourning Furūd. It is equally tempting, although not necessarily very original, to imagine that the room decorated with this hypothetical revetment would have been the setting for readings, recitations, and even re-enactments of the *Shāhnāma* story of Furūd and that the individual tiles served as points of reference or mnemonic devices for such performances.[22]

Now let us push this scenario of medieval *Shāhnāma* representation and *Shāhnāma* recital—that is, the visual and verbal—still further. The story of Furūd comes, as already mentioned, at the start of the *Shāhnāma* reign of Kay Khusraw and is followed by a half-dozen other tales that punctuate the perpetual warfare between Iran and Tūrān, a leitmotif of this part of Ferdowsi's epic.[23] One of these concerns the Iranian warrior Bīzhan, who actually took part in the expedition to Tūrān led by the rebellious commander Ṭūs and who was one of the two Iranians who ambushed and mortally wounded Furūd.[24] At a later moment in Kay Khusraw's reign, Bīzhan volunteers for a dangerous mission to rid lands on the Iranian-Tūrānian border of an invasion of wild boar. After successfully exterminating the marauding beasts, Bīzhan wanders across the border into Tūrān, where he meets and falls in love with Manīzha, the beautiful daughter of the despotic Tūrānian ruler Afrāsiyāb. Soon Manīzha's father learns of the lovers' disgraceful affair and has Bīzhan captured and chained in a pit sealed by an enormous stone. When news of this unfortunate turn of events gets back to Iran, Kay Khusraw employs his magic, world-revealing cup (the *jām-i gītī namā*) to locate the wayward warrior, and then dispatches a rescue mission led by Rostam who, with his superhuman strength, lifts the boulder off the pit and frees Bīzhan from captivity.[25]

As analyzed in careful detail by Charles Melville, this romantic adventure may be divided into five main episodes, each composed of a series of moments, some seventy-five altogether, which have been variously illustrated in *Shāhnāma* manuscripts.[26] By far the most frequently illustrated

22. A similar point has been made about the celebrated Freer Beaker, to be discussed below. See note 28 and Bloom and Blair, 1997, 271.

23. So the Kay Khusraw cycle is basically a frame story, encompassing other discrete narratives or *dāstāns*. See also the essay by Anna Krasnowolska in the present volume.

24. Davis 2000, 2:111–15.

25. Davis 2000, 2: 137–179.

26. Melville, 2006 and forthcoming. See also the *Shāhnāma* Project database.

moment in the story, and certainly the most dramatic moment of the tale, is when Rostam liberates Bīzhan from the pit. That this incident had artistic appeal before the start of the illustrated manuscript era is evidenced by a series of large luster-painted tiles.[27] Like the Furūd star tile, these doubtless would have formed part of wall revetments with extended narrative sequences, presumably three separate installations, although ones of later date and overall lesser quality than what we may imagine for the Furūd star tile. The same scene appears on a well-known ceramic drinking vessel (Figure 2) dating from the late twelfth or early thirteenth century (Freer Gallery of Art, Washington, D.C.). Like the contemporary star tile in Boston, the beaker is painted in the *mīnā'ī* technique and with great artistic verve. Unlike the star tile with its monoscenic decor, the beaker's is polyscenic, featuring a sequence of twelve incidents in the Bīzhan and Manīzha story, arranged in three superimposed registers, starting at the top with Kay Khusraw commissioning Bīzhan for the mission, continuing with Bīzhan being taken prisoner and imprisoned in the middle zone, and ending with Rostam rescuing Bīzhan at the bottom.

Elsewhere I have characterized the beaker's depiction as an epitomized pictorialization of the Bīzhan and Manīzha narrative as recounted by Ferdowsi, which gives the vessel a narrative turn as if it were a graphic novel or comic book, and seen it as a simulacrum for the world-revealing cup (the *jām-i gītī namā*) that Kay Khusraw used at the beginning of the new year (*now rūz*) to determine Bīzhan's whereabouts. I also have suggested that it was made for, or at least used on, a special occasion like a new year's celebration and passed around a convivial gathering while a storyteller recounted the Bīzhan and Manīzha tale.[28] Now I would like to pursue that possibility further and propose the following: that such a party would have been held in the hall decorated with tile revetments depicting the story of Furūd; that the Furūd story, with its defiant leadership, violent combats, and tragic ending, would have been recited first, with the guests following key narrative moments as represented on individual wall tiles; and, finally, that the Furūd performance would have been succeeded by a recitation or reading of the Bīzhan and Manīzha adventure, with its chivalric deeds, romantic encounter, and happy ending, as the guests followed its key moments as represented on the beaker while it was rotated and passed among the company.

What I envision here is nothing less than a total immersion in the Kay Khusraw cycle as recounted in Ferdowsi's *Shāhnāma*—a sort of medieval son et lumière—with the tiled wall revetments comprising the monumental

27. Watson 1985, 123–124; Brend and Melville 2010, cat. no. 12.

28. Simpson 1981, 2008 and 2012, and forthcoming.

Figure 2. Beaker, early 13th century, ceramic over-glaze painted with enamel. Courtesy Freer Gallery of Art, Smithsonian Institution, Washington, D.C., F1928.2.

mis-en-scène and the beaker the hand-held prop or accessory, and the two scales, major and minor, combining to convey and reinforce the epic's central themes of good versus evil, fathers versus sons, heroes versus kings, and all of mankind against its own mortality and the inevitability of fate. The poetic message could hardly have been lost on the party's host and guests, who may themselves have had a special identification either with Kay Khusraw, presented in the *Shāhnāma* as an ideal Persian monarch imbued with a strong ethical sensibility and endowed with *farr* (divine glory), or with Rostam, a paragon of heroism, strength, and loyalty, or even with Bīzhan, foolhardy perhaps but ever brave. To look upon the representation of such models of Persian princely and heroic virtues was both to celebrate Iran's glorious epic past and to strive to emulate or even to recreate it.[29]

To give a bit more historical and cultural context, or at least grounding, to what otherwise may seem like a fanciful scenario, let us return to the late thirteenth-century palace of Takht-i Solaymān, which today is the firmest point of archaeological reference for the decoration of Persian palaces with *Shāhnāma* imagery. As already mentioned, the surviving tilework from Takht-i Solaymān includes panels inscribed with *Shāhnāma* verses that would have belonged to the same frieze. As various scholars, starting with Gyuzalian, who first published these tiles, have noted, the molded tile verses come from the beginning of seven, presumably popular or especially memorable *Shāhnāma* stories, and probably were meant to be cues or aides-memoire of those particular epic tales.[30] It does not seem likely, therefore, that Ferdowsi's entire 50,000–60,000 verse poem was written out on the walls of Takht-i Solaymān. What the palace decor contained instead were verse selections from cycles belonging to the three main epic eras—mythical (Pishdadian), legendary (Kayanian), and historical (Sasanian)—through which Ferdowsi structured his account of Iran's "national" narrative.[31] So while the individual tile inscriptions were abbreviated, when installed side-by-side within a frieze at Takht-i Solaymān they filled the palace spaces with the full scope and continuum of Ferdowsi's epic poem.

By contrast with this broadly representative epigraphic expanse, the palace's figural imagery, at least what we know of it, seems to have been limited to two *Shāhnāma* stories and eras. The first example involves the conflict between Feridun and Zahhāk from Iran's mythical past.[32] The other image at Takht-i Solaymān comes from the *Shāhnāma*'s historical era and depicts the oft-repeated adventure of Bahrām Gūr at the hunt with his favorite

29. During the January 2011 *Shāhnāma* Seminar in Mumbai, Professor Olga Davidson raised the additional, and more ideologically charged, possibility that the original viewers of the Furud tile panel may have been concerned with issues of succession, as they contemplated the royal lineage passing from Kay Kāvūs to Siyāvush and from Siyāvush to Kay Khusraw and Furūd.

30. It is equally possible that the potter wrote out these verses as they were being read or recited by someone else. See Blair 2008, 162–163.

31. As Adamova 2010 observed, the specific verses on the Takht-i Solaymān tiles usually come from Ferdowsi's prelude to the *Shāhnāma* and from the beginnings of particular stories, and tend to describe natural features or evoke the moods and sentiments, with little or no mention of the names of any kings or heroes or of specific epic action or events.

32. Gonnella and Rauch 2011, cat. no. 81 (with earlier references). As previously noted (n. 10), there is a similar representation on an earlier fresco fragment, as well as other, quite well-known examples, on ceramic and metalwork vessels. Simpson 1985, 132–134, 143–144.

female companion, the harpist Āzāda.[33] This representation shows Bahrām Gūr mounted on his camel, with Āzāda behind, taking aim at a deer that is raising his hoof to scratch his nicked ear. The same scene also appears on a number of vessels, primarily bowls, painted in *mīnā'ī* technique and predating the construction and decoration of the Mongol palace. (So, to reiterate, what Takht-i Solaymān demonstrates is the continuation, and not the initiation, of a well-established visual narrative tradition.) Several such objects depict both Āzāda on the camel and Āzāda underneath the camel—that is, after Bahrām Gūr flings her down—thus conflating different moments of the story.[34] There is also a rare *mīnā'ī* relief tile decorated with Bahrām Gūr and Āzāda alone, which suggests that the deer might have appeared on the next tile in the frieze.[35]

What all this indicates is that *Shāhnāma* personages and *Shāhnāma* stories were ubiquitous in both the monumental and minor arts of medieval Iran, and that medieval Iranians of certain means and privilege were surrounded with *Shāhnāma* imagery of both large and small scale on a regular, and for some perhaps daily, basis. It is equally the case that the overall range of *Shāhnāma* imagery was extremely limited. Although it is possible that other epic scenes remain to be identified,[36] the iconographic corpus as we understand it today seems to be confined to one image representing the Feridun and Zahhāk story and thus the *Shāhnāma*'s entire mythical era, two scenes coming from the Kay Khusraw cycle and standing for the legendary era (the Iranians leaving Furūd's tomb and the story of Bīzhan and Manīzha), and one from the Bahrām Gūr cycle and so emblematic of the historical era. The reasons why medieval narrative iconography contained and medieval artists produced so few *Shāhnāma* images, albeit two that were regularly repeated (Feridun and Zahhāk, Bahrām Gūr and Āzāda), remain both intriguing and elusive, although it may be that further research into the reception of Ferdowsi's epic in the centuries immediately after its completion will shed some light on this art historical puzzle and that scholars will be in a better position to solve it by the time of the *Shāhnāma*'s next millennium.

33. Simpson 1985, 132–137, 144–146.

34. Simpson 1985, figs. 9 and 10; Brend and Melville 2010, cat. no. 16; see also Brooklyn Museum of Art, 86.227.11: http://www.brooklynmuseum.org/opencollection/objects/124989/Bowl_Depicting_Bahram_Gur_and_Azada

35. Simpson 1985, fig. 8.

36. E.g. on a fragmentary bowl in the Khalili Collection, proposed as representing the story of Feridun and his sons. See Brend and Melville 2010, cat. no. 15. The interior scene, however, shares iconographic elements with the Freer beaker, a similarity pursued in Simpson 2012. See also: Pancaroğlu, 110, 114 and fig. 71.

BIBLIOGRAPHY

Adamova, A. T. (2008), *Medieval Persian Painting: The Evolution of an Artistic Vision*, New York.

—— (2010), "Gyuzalian's works on the *Shahnama* in the light of today's knowledge," Presentation at a conference on *The Illustrated Shahnama*, London.

Arık, R. and Arık, O. (2008), *Tiles: Treasures of Anatolian Soil: Tiles of the Seljuk and Beylik Periods,* Istanbul.

Blair, S. S. (2008), "A Brief Biography of Abu Zayd," *Muqarnas* 25: 155–176.

Blair, S. S. and Bloom, J. M. (2006), *Cosmophilia: Islamic Art from The David Collection, Copenhagen*, Boston.

Bloom, J. and Blair, S. (1997), *Islamic Arts*, London.

Brend, B. and Melville, C. (2010), *Epic of the Persian Kings: The Art of Ferdowsi's Shahnameh*, Cambridge.

Carboni, S. and Masuya, T. (1993), *Persian Tiles*, New York.

Davis, D. (2000), *Stories from the Shahnameh of Ferdowsi 2: Fathers and Sons*, Washington, D.C.

Ettinghausen, R. (1977), *Arab Painting*, New York.

Gemeente Museum (1927), *Tentoonstelling van Islamische Kunst*, 'S-Gravenhage.

Gonnella, J. and Rauch, Christoph (2011), *Heroische Zeiten: Tausend Jahre persisches Buch der Könige*, Berlin.

Gyuzalian, L. (1949), "Frieze tiles of the thirteenth-century with poetical inscriptions," *Epigrafika vostoka* 3: 72–81.

—— (1951), "Verses from the *Shāhnāme* on 13th–14th century ceramics," *Epigrafika vostoka* 4: 39–55.

—— (1952), "Verses from the *Shāhnāme* on 13th–14th century ceramics," *Epigrafika vostoka* 5: 33–50.

Hall, A. R. (1934), "A New Collection of Islamic Pottery," *Museum of Fine Arts Bulletin* 32, Boston: 58–67.

Khaleghi-Motlagh, D., ed. (1992), *Abu'l Qasem Ferdowsi, Shahnameh* 3, New York.

Khaleghi-Motlagh, D. (2001), "Forud," in: *EIr* X, 107a-b.

Komaroff, L. and Carboni, S., eds. (2002), *The Legacy of Genghis Khan*, New York.

Koss, K., McCarthy, B., et al. (2009), "Analysis of Persian Painted *Minai* Ware," in: B. McCarthy, E. S. Chase, et al. (eds.), *Scientific Research on Historic Asian Ceramics: Proceedings of the Fourth Forbes Symposium at the Freer Gallery of Art*, London, 33–47.

Masuya, T. (2002), "Ilkhanid Courtly Life," in: L. Komoroff and S. Carboni (eds.), *The Legacy of Genghis Khan: Courtly Art and Culture in Western Asia, 1256–1353*, New York, 74–103.

Melikian-Chirvani, A. S. (1984), "Le *Shāh-Nāme,* la gnose soufie et le pouvoir mongol," *Journal Asiatique* 272: 249–338.

—— (1988), "Le Livre des Rois, Miroir du Destin," *Studia Iranica* 17: 7–46.

—— (1991), "Le Livre des Rois, Miroir du Destin. II–Takhte Soleymān et la symbolique du *Shāh-Nāme,*" *Studia Iranica* 20: 33–148.

—— (1996), *Les frises du Shāh Nāme dans l'architecture iranienne sous les IlKhān*, Paris.

—— (1997), "Conscience du Passé et Résistance Culturelle dans l'Iran Mongol," in: D. Aigle (ed.), *L'Iran face à la Domination Mongole*, Tehran.

Melville, C. (2006), "Text and Image in the Story of Bizhan and Manizha: I," in: C. Melville (ed.), *Shahnama Studies I*, Cambridge, 71–96.

—— (forthcoming), "Text and Image in the Story of Bizhan and Manizha: II."

O'Kane, B. (2009), *The Appearance of Persian on Islamic* Art, New York.

Pinder-Wilson, R. (1957), *Islamic Art*, New York.

O'Kane, B. (2007), "The Uses of Captions in Medieval Literary Arabic Manuscripts," in: A. Contadini (ed.), *Arab Painting: Text and Image in Illustrated Arabic Manuscripts*, Leiden and Boston,137–144.

Pancaroğlu, O. (2007), *Perpetual Glory: Medieval Islamic Ceramics from the Harvey B. Plotnick Collection*, Chicago.

Pope, A. U. and Ackerman, P., eds. (1938–39), *A Survey of Persian Art* 5, London and New York.

Pope, A. U. and Ackerman, P. (1945), *Masterpieces of Persian Art*, New York.

Roxburgh, D. J., ed. (2005), *Turks: A Journey of a Thousand Years, 600–1600*, London.

Shahnama Project database: http://shahnama.caret.cam.ac.uk/new/jnama/index/depiction

Simpson, M. S. (1979), *The Illustration of an Epic: The Earliest Shahnama Manuscripts*, New York and London.

—— (1981), "The Narrative Structure of a Medieval Iranian Beaker," *Ars Orientalis* 12: 15–24.

—— (1985), "Narrative Allusion and Metaphor in the Decoration of Medieval Islamic Objects," in: M. S. Simpson and H. Kessler (eds.), *Studies in the History of Art* 16: *Pictorial Narrative in Antiquity and the Middle Ages*, Washington, D.C., 131–149.

—— (2004), "*Shahnama* as Text and *Shahnama* as Image," in: R. Hillenbrand (ed.), *Shahnama: The Visual Language of the Persian Book of Kings*, Aldershot, Hants, 9–25.

—— (2008 & 2012), "Notions of Narrativity in Persian Imagery, or Giving the Freer Beaker a Narrative Turn," Presentation at the First Biennial Symposium (2008), Historians of Islamic Art Association, Philadelphia; expanded version at the Islamic Research Seminar (2012), Oxford.
—— (2009–12), "*Šah-Nāma* iv: Illustrations," in: *EIr* online, http://www.iranicaonline.org/articles/sah-nama-iv-illustrations
—— (2012), "The Cosmic Cup in Medieval and Later Persian Art," Khalili Memorial Lecture, London.
—— (forthcoming), "A Medieval Representation of Kay Khosrow's *jam-e giti nama*," in: R. Hillenbrand, A. C. S. Peacock and F. Abdullaeva (eds.), *Ferdowsi, The Mongols and Iranian History: Art, Literature and Culture from Early Islam to Qajar Persia*, London.
Sims, E. (2002), *Peerless Images: Persian Painting and its Sources*, New Haven and London.
Watson, O. (1985), *Persian Lustre Ware*, London and Boston.
—— (1975), "The Masjidi 'Alī, Quhrūd: Architectural and Epigraphic Survey," *Iran* 13: 59–74.

The Production of Mughal *Shāhnāmas*
Imperial, Sub-Imperial, and Provincial Manuscripts

Sunil Sharma
Boston University

In keeping with the Persianate nature of courtly culture in India during the Mughal era, familiarity with the canon of classical Persian literature was a standard feature of the education of princes and noblemen. Their reading lists would have included classics such as the *dīvāns* of the poets Anvarī (d. 1189) and Hāfiz (d. 1379), the *khamsas* of Nizāmī (d. ca. 1209) and Amīr Khusraw (d. 1325), the various *masnavīs* of Jāmī (d. 1492) and, of course, Firdawsī's (d. 1020) *Shāhnāma*, completed in CE 1010. While selections from most of these works were read, copied, and imitated chiefly for their literary and artistic value, the *Shāhnāma* is believed to have held a symbolic significance in the life of Persianate courts. The reason why this epic achieved this lofty status is explained by Charles Melville: "A consequence of the *Shāhnāma*'s preoccupation with kingship and legitimacy is a perception of the political relevance of the work to later rulers, who in turn sought to exploit it as propaganda for their own dynastic aspirations."[1] Not all courts and dynastic houses, especially in Persianate India, may have held the same attitude towards this text. The Mughals, for instance, emphasized their connections with their Timurid Turko-Iranian past, of which the *Shāhnāma* was a part, on the one hand, and sought to integrate themselves into Indian culture by patronizing translations of Sanskrit literary works on the other. Thus, the position of the *Shāhnāma* among the Mughals is a complex subject that cannot be treated in a monolithic fashion. In order to address the problem of Mughal *Shāhnāmas*, instead of focusing solely on imperial copies of the epic it is necessary to study the entire spectrum of Mughal illustrated manuscripts of the text.

Som Prakash Verma has noted that "some of the Persian favorites that were repeatedly illustrated in Central Asia and Western Asia find little place in the imperial Mughal atelier. A case in point is the *Shāhnāma* of Firdawsi, of which no illustrated manuscript from the Imperial Mughal school is

1. Melville 2006, xxii.

known."[2] Whether entirely true or not, there was an evident lack of imperial attention to Firdawsī's work during the early Mughal age, while the same period witnessed a proliferation of so-called sub-imperial or popular copies of the epic. The term "popular Mughal art," coined by Pramod Chandra "to denote the breadth of its class of patrons and its derivative relationship to imperial Mughal painting," is the most useful one for classifying the many non-imperial Mughal *Shāhnāmas*.[3] According to John Seyller, popular Mughal painting "consists primarily of illustrated manuscripts of the classics of Persian literature;"[4] thus the appropriateness of this term for the *Shāhnāma*. Other terms such as "provincial Mughal" and "sub-imperial Mughal" are also in use but can be problematic due to the overlap between the two categories.[5] The latter is used for works that are "firmly or plausibly associated with members of the Mughal nobility," but such patrons could also have been located in the provinces and not necessarily in the imperial capitals of Agra, Delhi or Lahore.

Early Mughal Period

Illustrated copies of the *Shāhnāma* appeared in India from at least the fifteenth century, if not earlier, although only a few folios of such works have been recorded.[6] According to Marianna Shreve Simpson, "Indian admiration for the *Šāh-nāma* remained strong during the Mughal period, particularly among the dynasty's early rulers."[7] The *Shāhnāma* produced for the Timurid prince Muhammad Jūkī in ca. 1444 was a prized Mughal copy and bears the ownership seals of five emperors, including those of Bābur (r. 1526-30), who originally brought the manuscript from Herat to India, Shāh Jahān (r. 1628-58), whose hand-written note about the manuscript entering the royal library on the day of his accession to the throne is included, all the way to 'Ālamgīr (r. 1658-1707) (Figure 1).[8] Such books, therefore, were an important component of Mughal pride: "Th[e] treasure trove of Timurid books, like

2. Verma 2002, 157.

3. Seyller 1999, 24; also footnote 18 on page 40.

4. Seyller 1999, 32.

5. The term "provincial Mughal" was first used by Barrett and Gray 1963, while "sub-imperial Mughal" was coined by Archer 1960; Seyller 1999, 24; footnotes 19-20, 40.

6. For an argument for illustrated *Shāhnāmas* appearing in India beginning in the first half of the fourteenth century, see Robinson 1983, 280-81; for a discussion of a possible Indian provenance of the so-called Gutman *Shāhnāma*, see Swietochowski 1994, 80; also see Brac de la Perrière 2008.

7. Simpson 2012.

8. Brand and Lowry 1985, 88.

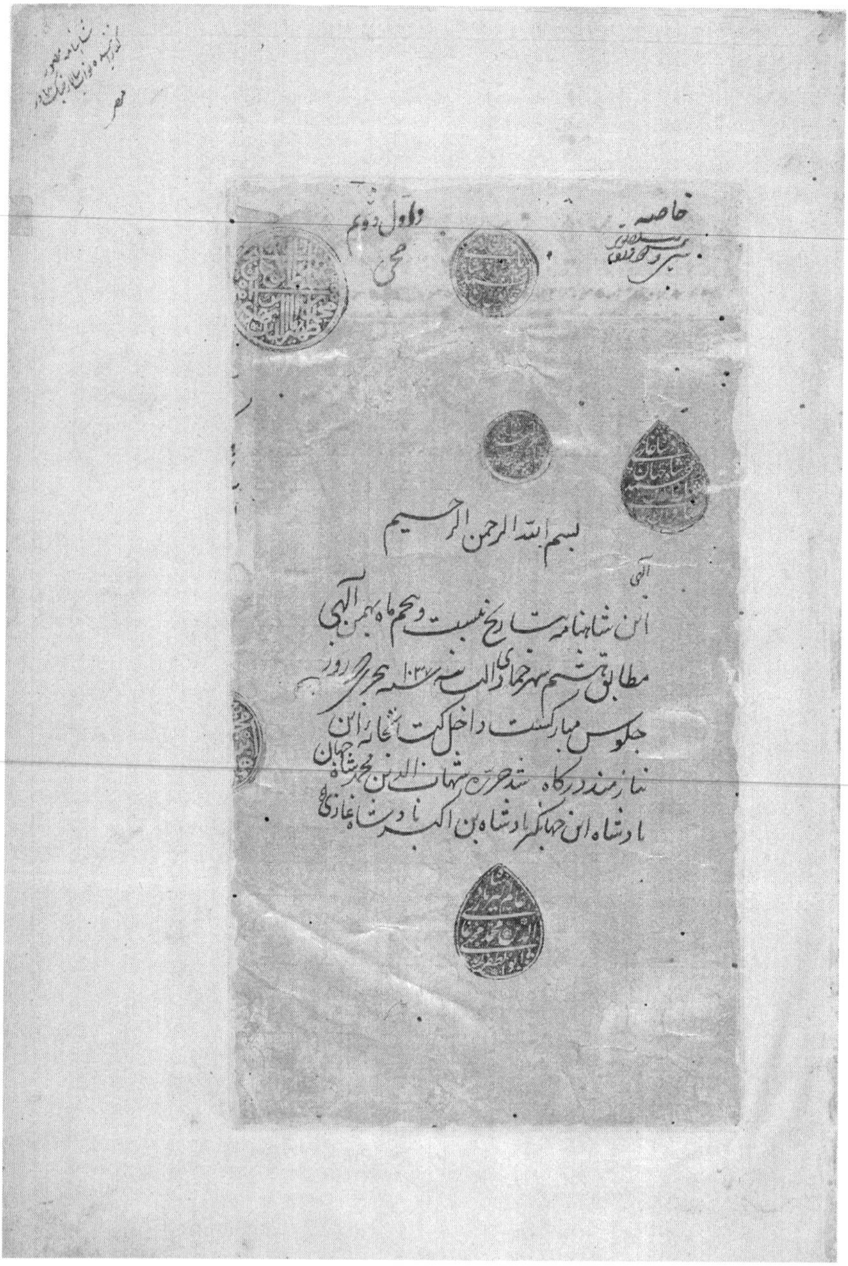

Figure 1. Jūkī *Shāhnāma*. RAS Persian MS 239, f. 536b. Reproduced by permission of the Royal Asiatic Society of Great Britain and Ireland, London.

crown jewels, were perceived as part of the ruling elites' imperial charisma: symbols of current role and reminders of a fabled past."[9] Notwithstanding the paucity of newly produced imperial *Shāhnāmas*, there is sufficient evidence that several members of the Mughal royal family and nobility owned copies produced in Iran.[10]

In addition, there are a few examples of Mughal gift-giving that involved the *Shāhnāma*. In his memoirs, Jahāngīr writes that in 1622, "I viewed the *Shāhnāma* [of Firdawsī] and a *khamsa* of Shaykh Nizāmī illustrated by master painters, along with other presents, sent by Mustafā Khān, governor of Thatta, as an offering."[11] Another such gift is a large, illustrated *Shāhnāma* manuscript that was personally presented to the Emperor Shāh Jahān by 'Alī Mardān Khān, a Safavid nobleman, who defected to the Mughals in 1637 after their victory over Qandahar and who was later governor of Kabul and Kashmir.[12] A *Shāhnāma* from the city of Shiraz in Fars province was perhaps gifted to Shāh Jahān and then to Prince Murād; the latter owned it by 1646 at the latest, and subsequently it was in the possession of one of 'Ālamgīr's officials.[13] From all this we may surmise that there must have been scores of such *Shāhnāma* manuscripts in circulation all over the pre-modern Persianate world.[14]

As for the actual patronage and production of *Shāhnāma* manuscripts in early Mughal India, it has been suggested that the Timurid treasure known today as the Muhammad Jūkī *Shāhnāma* may have inspired the third Mughal emperor, Akbar (r. 1556-1605), to commission his own copy of the *Shāhnāma* in 1582, as a way of connecting with "past royal glory and asserting his authority and rule."[15] Akbar's court historian 'Abd al-Qādir Badā'ūnī does record the production of a copy of the Persian epic in the early years of Akbar's reign, although he does not specify whether this was an illustrated copy. This supposedly lost (or perhaps still to be located) copy of the *Shāhnāma* has long intrigued modern scholars and has led some to propose at least five dispersed paintings as being of Akbari provenance. These are introduced briefly in an appendix in the context of whether they necessar-

9. Lentz and Lowry 1989, 321.

10. One such work is described by Stanley 2004, 85-87.

11. Jahāngīr, *Jahāngīrnāma*, 392. All translations are mine unless otherwise indicated.

12. This manuscript is in the Khuda Bakhsh Library, Patna, and is described by Marshall 1985, no 472, 147.

13. "It seems likely that the *Shahnama* was confiscated by 'Alamgir when Muradbakhsh was arrested, since the first annotation by one of his officials was made on 15 October 1658," Stanley 2004, 87.

14. There have been few studies of the movement of manuscripts during this period.

15. Simpson 2012.

ily belonged to Firdawsī's version of the *Shāhnāma* or to an abridgment, or perhaps even an album.

Three of the five paintings in the appendix (1, 4, 5) do not have any text on them, while the other two (2, 3) have text panels that are either blank or appear to have been erased. The existence of prose text (3) challenges the common assumption that it was Firdawsī's work that was commissioned or read at Akbar's court. As discussed below, there were several other prose or mixed prose-verse abridgments in existence that these paintings could have illustrated. Of course, all of these five Akbar-period paintings may not have been part of the same manuscript, and it is also possible that they may have been in an album, rather than a manuscript, which included scenes from the *Shāhnāma*. But if there was an Akbari *Shāhnāma*, its disappearance raises all sorts of complicated questions about its fate.[16] In any case, the production of an Akbari *Shāhnāma* must be seen in the larger literary context of the late sixteenth-century Mughal court, and it is possible that there were multiple copies of the *Shāhnāma* transcribed and illustrated in Akbar's time.

Mughal sources note Akbar's interest in having the *Shāhnāma* copied in the royal atelier. There is also a reference to his interest in this book of stories as purely a work of entertainment with didactic value. In the list of books that the Emperor Akbar was fond of listening to, the historian Abū al-Fazl includes the *Shāhnāma* among other Persian classics:

> The *Akhlāq-i Nāsirī* [by Ṭūsī], the *Kīmiyā-yi Sa'ādat* [by Ghazālī], the *Qābūsnāma*, the letters of Sharaf Manerī, the *Gulistān* [by Sa'dī], the *Hadīqa* by Hakīm Sanā'ī, the *Mathnavī-i ma'navī* [by Rūmī], the *Jām-i Jam* [by Awhadī], the *Būstān* [by Sa'dī], the *Shāhnāma* [by Firdawsī], the *khamsa* of Shaykh Nizāmī, the *kullīyāts* of [Amīr] Khusraw and Mawlana Jāmī, the *dīvāns* of Khāqānī, Anvarī, and other history books are read out to him.[17]

Over time, as the Mughals expanded the frontiers of their empire and became more multicultural, Akbar's interest shifted to the Indian, i.e. Sanskrit, classics.[18] Badā'ūnī provides the chronology and motivation for the

16. In a popular Mughal *Shāhnāma* dating from the late sixteenth or early seventeenth century, now in the Royal Asiatic Society (Codrington no. 241), there is a painting of Zāl and his father Sām in distinctive dress and head-dress; according to Digby 1979, "the iconology of the scene may contain a reference to the restoration of his son and heir Akbar to the emperor Humāyūn after the reconquest of Kābul in A.D. 1544," in which case, "the representation must surely derive from the missing, probably dispersed, *Shāh-nāma* illustrated for the imperial library of Akbar," 113.

17. Abū al-Fazl, *Ā'īn-i Akbarī*, 96.

18. Ali 1992, 38-45.

large-scale projects of manuscript production and translation in the royal atelier; here he discusses the circumstances leading to the translation of the *Mahābhārata*:

> When he [Akbar] had had the *Shāhnāma* and the tale of Amīr Hamza copied in seventeen volumes over fifteen years, with much gold spent in illuminating them, likewise he repeatedly heard the story of Abū Muslim, the *Jāmi' al-hikāyāt*, and others. He realized that most of these [works] were poetry and fiction, but since they were composed at an auspicious hour and their star was passing, they received great fame. Now he ordered Indian books, written by wise ascetics and which were all correct and decisive texts, being the axis of the religion, beliefs and worship of this group. It was thus written in the preface of those books, "Why should I not have them done in my name for they are novel and fresh, and they will produce fruits of felicity, both temporal and spiritual, and lead to undying pomp and glory and an abundance of children and wealth."[19]

Akbar's atelier was occupied with the large-scale *Hamzanāma* project during the years 1558-72.[20] Thus, according to Badā'ūnī's narrative, the now-lost *Shāhnāma* must have been produced during the same years. It is not clear, of course, whether it was illustrated on the same grand scale as the *Hamzanāma*. The translation of the Sanskrit classics began a decade after the production of these manuscripts. The *Mahābhārata* was translated during the years 1582-84 with the participation of Naqīb Khān and the reluctant historian Badā'ūnī, and the imperial illustrated manuscript was executed in 1586. The translation and manuscript production of the *Rāmāyana* was begun in 1584 and finished in 1588-91, about which Badā'ūnī writes that this is "a superior composition to the *Mahabharata*,"[21] but that "it is clear that either these events are not true, and this is a mere tale and pure imagination, like the *Shāhnāma*, and the stories of *Amīr Hamza*, or else they must have happened in the time of the dominion of the beasts and the *jinns*."[22]

Badā'ūnī's attitude suggests that all literary works on the subject of epic and adventure were lumped together as fiction. Indeed, even those people who were favorably disposed towards one tradition or the other would have been aware that the Sanskrit and Persian epics shared elements in common. In comparing illustrations from manuscripts of epics from the two traditions, Mughal/Indo-Persian and Safavid/Iranian, one finds an almost identical

19. *Muntakhab al-tavārīkh*, 2: 223.
20. Detailed essays about this project can be found in Seyller 2002.
21. *Muntakhab al-tavārīkh*, 2: 234.
22. *Muntakhab al-tavārīkh*, 2: 235.

Figure 2. Rāma and Laksmana Confront the Demons Mārīca and Subāhu. *Rāmāyana* of Valmiki, Freer Gallery of Art, Smithsonian Institution, Washington, D.C.: Gift of Charles Lang Freer, F1907.271.38b.

Figure 3. Rustam Carried by the Dīv Akvān about to be Thrown into the Sea. *Shāhnāma* (Book of Kings) of Firdausi, 1660's. Painting by Mu'in Musavvir, active ca. 1630-97. 1974.290.43, folio 158v, Image © The Metropolitan Museum of Art. Image source: Art Resource, NY.

representation of demons, Indian *rākshasas* and Persian *dīvs* (Figures 2 & 3), indicating that some of the iconography of the separate traditions had fused together in the Mughal imagination.[23] This was, of course, part of Akbar's program for a dialogue of religious communities that was executed at a literary and visual level.

Later Mughal Period

At the beginning of the emperor Jahāngīr's reign (r. 1605-27), when the prospects of large projects from his father's time had dried up, many artists from the imperial atelier found themselves working on a freelance basis or for provincial patrons. According to Asok Kumar Das, unemployed artists, "even entire families of artists, moved to the courts of the Mughal governors, generals and of other high-ranging officials."[24] John Seyller suggests that the move away from the imperial workshop had begun earlier:

> [W]hether for reasons of social fashion, conspicuous self-promotion, or sincere interest in literature and painting, some members of the Mughal nobility and merchant class set out to imitate imperial sponsorship of the arts, and began to collect and commission the same types of manuscripts produced in the imperial atelier.[25]

From 1590 to 1620 imperial artists found themselves working for Mughal nobility in or outside the imperial capital. On the basis of Seyller's study of non-imperial paintings from this period, it seems "likely that these manuscripts were neither commissioned individually nor produced by a stable body of artists. They appear to be the perfunctory products of a commercial atelier, whose members were probably newly itinerant artists working in the vicinity of Agra."[26] Thus, there is evidence for the production of non-imperial copies of the *Shāhnāma*, among other texts, from the late sixteenth century onwards, with their artists and owners having some connection to the Mughal court. Regional courts of local rulers or nobles, or Mughal princes and officials posted in the provinces, would have attracted such artists. Perhaps groups of people who were newly educated in Persianate learning in cities and town also commissioned manuscripts on a modest scale.

The case of a *Shāhnāma* (British Library Add. 5600) owned by the Mughal general and man of letters 'Abd al-Rahīm Khān-i khānān is an example

23. For *divs* in Iranian culture and art, see Leoni 2008.
24. Das 2005, 5-6.
25. Seyller 1999, 23.
26. Seyller 1999, 33.

of a manuscript that started life in the imperial atelier and ended up being completed in a non-imperial setting (Figure 4). In 1613 it was presented by the emperor Jahāngīr to a certain Allāhvardī Chelā, who in turn gave it to Khvāja Muhammad Rashīd, who passed it on to the Khān-i khānān. In 1616 it was refurbished in the latter's workshop and the over-painting of some of its images has been described by Seyller as "one of the most fascinating cases of the renovation of damaged or incomplete manuscripts in Mughal painting studios."[27] In addition to the over-painted pages, this manuscript includes newly executed paintings.[28] The text was more important than the paintings in this case since the Khān-i khānān "was generally content to experience paintings through the mediation of literature, and displayed a relative indifference to the power of images in their own right."[29] Sanskrit classics, such as the *Rāmāyana*, *Mahābhārata*, and the *Rāgamālā*, as well as Persian texts such as the *Khamsa* of Amīr Khusraw and Hātifī's *Timurnāma*, were all illustrated in the Khān-i khānān's workshop, showing the eclectic nature of the patron's literary taste. A transition from imperial to sub-imperial, such as the British Library *Shāhnāma* reveals, would also naturally have resulted in the creation of provincial copies of Firdawsī's poem as Mughal princes, governors, and other nobility posted in various provinces imitated the trends in the imperial capitals and used local artists and calligraphers.

Jahāngīr's reign witnessed a turn towards everything Iranian, from the prevailing trends in Persian literature to the appointment of grandees at court.[30] As a result, there must have been a serious interest in the *Shāhnāma* at the imperial level. Given their ornate gold margins, two *Shāhnāma* paintings dating from around 1610 were probably commissioned by Jahāngīr.[31] While stylistically similar to sub-imperial compositions, the "lively and unusually colourful" character of these paintings, as, for example, Feridun striking down Zahhāk (Los Angeles County Museum of Art M. 78.9.5), executed by the artist Dhanrāj, who had previously worked on several Akbari manuscripts,[32] makes them likely products of the imperial atelier at the "height of the fashion for Persian-influenced works"[33] At the same time that

27. Seyller 1999, 264; also see Qureshi 2012 for a comparative study of a manuscript with later paintings from Akhbar's reign.

28. In addition to Seyller, also see Brend 2010, 226. Another instance of the retouching of an Akbari period sub-imperial *Shāhnāma* is described in Leach 1995, 670.

29. Seyller 1999, 314.

30. The reason for this change was chiefly owing to the political and cultural influence of the empress Nūr Jahān, who was of Iranian origin.

31. Leach 1995, 581. According to Brend 2010, however, "No *Shahnameh* is known to have been made for Jahangir," 53.

32. Leach 1995, 80.

33. Leach 1986, 78.

Figure 4. Zāl in Rudabā's Pavilion. Painter: Qasim, c. 1616. British Library, Add. 5600, f. 42b.

Figure 5. Rustam and the Akvān Dīv. CBL In 47.10. © The Trustees of The Chester Beatty Library, Dublin.

such Persianate-style paintings were in vogue, there is also evidence for the existence of an Indian-oriented trend in *Shāhnāma* painting, as in the image of Akavān and Rustam (Chester Beatty Library In 47.10)[34] (Figure 5). This striking and unique representation of Akavān *dīv* as an elephant continues the trend of blending Indian and Persian iconography in Akbari paintings and perfectly signifies the *Shāhnāma*'s principle value in Mughal society: as a book of tales that resonated with Indian stories drawn from Sanskrit literature.

Shāhnāma Imitations, Abridgments and Prose Adaptations

It is relevant here that imitations of Firdawsī's epic were also produced by poets at Persianate courts in India, substituting the martial victories of contemporaneous figures for the exploits of traditional heroes.[35] According to Badā'ūnī, a poet named Manzarī Samarqandī planned to compose one of the many pseudo-*Shāhnāmas*, i.e. a continuation or imitation of Firdawsī's poem, and wrote several tales, including one on the battle between Sikandar Sūr and the Mughals. Apparently, the Mughal general and courtier Bayram Khān suggested some corrections on it to the poet, who in one night revised the poem of 300-400 couplets and in the morning recited it in an assembly.[36] The interest in contemporary history especially appealed to the emperor Shāh Jahān, whose court poets produced at least three *Shāhnāma*-like epics to honor him, parts of which may have been read aloud in his presence. During Shāh Jahān's reign, imperial energies were directed towards producing epics in which the hero was the emperor himself.[37] These works, however, are only related in poetic form to the *Shāhnāma* and cannot be considered spinoffs of the original tales.

Several condensed versions of the *Shāhnāma*, in prose or mixed prose-verse, also were composed in pre-Mughal and Mughal India. These usually included stories from the mythological and heroic sections of the epic that were popular in India, but omitted the more obscure historical parts dealing with the Sasanians. The compilation of an early abridgment of the epic,

34. Leach 1995, 581. Another instance of such a cultural blending is the depiction of the early Iranian king Hūshang before a Hindu shrine with three yogis in a Deccani copy of an abridged *Shāhnāma*, Leach 1995, 904-905.

35. For the general phenomenon of epics inspired by the *Shāhnāma*, see Sharma 2003, 112-8.

36. *Muntakhab al-tavārīkh*, 3: 233.

37. Losty 1982, 85. Examples of such poems are Kalīm's *Shahanshāhnāma* and Qudsī's *Zafarnāmah-yi Shāhjahānī*. These non-illustrated works have not been studied from a textual point of view.

called the *Ikhtiyārāt-i Shāhnāma*, was probably wrongly attributed to the late Ghaznavid poet Mas'ūd Sa'd Salmān (d. 1121).[38] During the early years of the Delhi Sultanate, the poet 'Awfī compiled the *Javāmi' al-hikāyāt*, a compendium of stories from Islamic lore, including some from the *Shāhnāma*, for al-Junaydī, the vizier of Iltutmish (r. 1210-36). A fifteenth-century manuscript of this text, perhaps from Bidar (Deccan), survives today (British Library, Or. 11676),[39] along with another abridgment in a seventeenth-century manuscript from Golconda in the Deccan (Chester Beatty Library, In 23).[40] The *Intikhāb-i Shāhnāma* (New York Public Library, Spencer, Indo-Pers. Ms. 1) was copied in 1501 by Muhammad Mu'tabar Badakhshī in Jaunpur, a small sultanate that was annexed by the Mughals in 1559. The paintings in this manuscript were added later, although Barbara Schmitz suggests that the manuscript could be of a later date and points out the random order of the selections and the lack of correlation between text and image in ten of the miniatures.[41]

Further regarding the Mughal renditions of Firdawsī's poetry into prose, Badā'ūnī writes that in CE 1595, "Mullā Taqī of Shus[h]tar joined, who considers himself to be the most learned of the learned, and by order [of the emperor] is engaged in rendering the *Shahnāma* into prose."[42] Of all the Indian abridgments of the Persian epic, the *Tārīkh-i dilgushā-yi Shamshīrkhānī*, dating from CE 1653 and written for the Mughal governor of Ghazni, Shamsher Beg, is the best known and survives in multiple copies.[43] Its author, Tavakkul Beg, writes in the introduction, "Both the reader and listener get bored reading and listening to the *Shāhnāma*, especially men of governance, who are always occupied with matters of the state and important affairs, have little time to read books."[44] From this we may infer that there were all kinds of *Shāhnāma* texts in circulation in Mughal India, and that individual paintings did not necessarily originate with Firdawsī's text.

For the late Mughal period, too, there is scant information to gauge the imperial interest in Firdawsī's poem. Regarding a copy of the *Shāhnāma* made for the Emperor Shāh 'Ālam II (r. 1759-1806), who ruled during a time of political and social upheaval, Linda York Leach describes its production

38. de Blois 1992, 152-153.

39. Brend 2010, 217; Losty 1982, 58.

40. Leach 1995, 904-905.

41. Schmitz 1992, 219-221.

42. *Muntakhab al-tavārīkh*, 2: 283. Copies of this work have not been identified so far.

43. de Blois 1992, 153-5; also see Khan 2012 for more on this work and the fate of the *Shāhnāma* in later Mughal times.

44. Tavakkul Beg, *Tārīkh-i dilgushā*,15; The original Persian is as follows: *az khvāndan va shunūdan-i ān qārī va sāmī' ra imlāl dast dihad, khusūsan ahl-i hukūmat rā kih hamīsha dar tadbīr-i mamlikat va muham-i subadārī ishtighāl dārand va fursat-i mutāli'a-yi kutub, kamtar rūy dihad.*

as "a desperate pretence of status," adding that the work "may have been produced in order to impress visitors to the court, some of whom may have been influential in reporting to the British."[45] A most unusual copy is a stylistically hybrid *Shāhnāma,* dating from 1695, that was commissioned by a Mughal official who was temporarily stationed in the Kangra hills.[46]

It would appear that the ultimate destiny of the *Shāhnāma* in the eighteenth and nineteenth centuries was as an export item that was produced by the dozen in Srinagar and Lahore, much like the handicrafts of Kashmir today, for domestic and international markets. The evidence for this may be gleaned from an unpublished work by William Moorcroft who, in the years 1819-25, made a survey of the crafts of Kashmir. Moorcroft noted that there were around 700 to 800 copyists preparing commissioned manuscripts. He wrote that "they transcribe the Quran, Firdausi's *Shāhnāma*, and a very small number of other books that are the objects of a small but regular trade." In Schmitz's view the tastes of the book buyers in Lahore were "much more catholic." The scribes in Lahore produced Qurans and *Shāhnāmas* in addition to scientific and technical works, as well as Persian literary works, including those translated from Indian languages.[47] Thus, the process of producing popular *Shāhnāmas* that had begun when Akbari artists started working around the Mughal capital on a freelance basis continued in a new setting in the provinces of Kashmir and Punjab.

Conclusion

The *Shāhnāma* did not have the same cultural associations for various groups of non-Muslim Indians as the *Rāmāyana* and *Mahābhārata*. In fact, and as discussed above, even Persianate Indian Muslims and Hindus often viewed it as "just" a book of stories. In Iranian lands the epic was more strongly connected to national identity than in Mughal India, although for obvious reasons the large contingent of Iranians and Central Asians at the court of the emperors Jahāngīr and Shāh Jahān would have been more attached to Firdawsī's text. Another group in India that would have a similar relationship to the work would have been Zoroastrian Parsis, but their contribution to the production of copies of the *Shāhnāma* is outside the Mughal cultural sphere.

In the end, what did the *Shāhnāma* signify for the Mughals? As Ebba Koch explains, "Confronted with the vastness and complexity of their empire and

45. Leach 1998, 155. The manuscript with 28 miniatures is described on 155-156; also see Brend 2012, 234-237.

46. Leach 1995, 1034-1042.

47. Lafont and Schmitz 2002, 98.

its heterogeneous traditions, the Mughals felt a greater need to measure and support their imperial authority with a carefully constructed image of rulers. Each emperor found his own means of translating this image into the arts, while building on the tradition of those who preceded him."[48] Thus, various texts had different symbolic valences for the Mughals and the wider literary culture of translation of Sanskrit epics and the complexities of readership and literary and artistic tastes in Persianate India must be taken into consideration while studying individual *Shāhnāma* manuscripts from the Mughal period.

Appendix

1. Rūdāba lets down her hair for Zāl to climb up (Figure 6). Keir Collection, London.

Skelton believes that this well-known painting, dated c. 1580, "formed part of a copy of the ... *Shāhnāma* made for the Emperor Akbar's library."[49] The painting contains no text and the folio has been remounted at a later date and so lacks its original borders.

2. Kayūmars enthroned. Present whereabouts unknown.

The quality of this painting relates to Akbar-period painting, although, as Skelton has observed, there is a discrepancy in size between this work and the one in the Keir Collection.[50] Nonetheless, "this does not rule out the possibility that the two compositions formed part of the same manuscript."[51] A small text box at the lower left of the painting is blank.

3. Bahrām Gūr Kills Lions and Seizes the Crown (Figure 7). Museum of Fine Arts, Boston, 14.648.[52]

Skelton notes that the painting's text is "clearly not from the *Shāhnāma* but from a prose historical work" and questions its origin as from an Akbari *Shāhnāma*.[53] The faint script in the text box, perhaps deliberately erased, is clearly prose, and so definitely not from a copy of Firdawsī's text. The museum now identifies it as a scene from Bal'amı's *History of Ṭabarı*. The painting, however, shares features of Akbar-period style.

48. Koch 2001, 162. Rizvi 2012 provides a comparative view of how the text was viewed and used by the Safavids in Iran.

49. Skelton 1976, 237-238.

50. Sotheby's 1967, 39.

51. Skelton 1976, 238.

52. Coomaraswamy 1930, 6: 18-19.

53. Skelton 1976, 238.

Figure 6. Rūdāba lets down her hair for Zāl to climb up. Keir Collection, London.

4. Zāl in the *sīmurgh*'s nest. Private collection.

This painting has no text. Welch dates it to the time the emperor Humāyūn was in Kabul (1550-55) and suggests that it is the work of the Safavid artist Mīr Sayyid 'Alī.[54]

5. Rostam and Rakhsh wounded in combat with Isfandīyār. British Museum 1920.0917.

This painting comes from a Mughal album dated to the 1590s. According to Barbara Brend, "Possibly from a *Shāhnāma* for Akbar, the picture has experienced considerable repainting and patching, faces perhaps receiving attention before landscape."[55]

54. Published in Welch 2004, 36. I would like to thank Dr. Laura E. Parodi for sharing her thoughts on the subject. She also dates this painting stylistically to Akbar's atelier.

55. Melville and Brend 2010, no. 95, 222-223.

Figure 7. Bahrām Gūr Kills Lions and Seizes the Crown. Bal'amī's *History of Ṭabarī*: Museum of Fine Arts, Boston Frances Bartlett Donation of 1912 and Picture Fund, 14.648. Photograph © 2013, Museum of Fine Arts, Boston.

Bibliography

Abū al-Fazl (2005), *Ā'īn-i Akbarī*, Sir Sayyid Ahmad (ed.), 3 vols., Aligarh: Aligarh Muslim University.

Ali, M. Athar (1992), "Translations of Sanskrit Works at Akbar's Court," *Social Scientist*, v. 20, no. 9/10: 38-45.

Badā'ūnī, 'Abd al-Qādir (2000-2001), *Muntakhab al-tavārīkh*, Mawlavī Ahmad (ed.), 'Alī Sāhib and Tawfiq Subhānī, 3 vols., Tehran: Anjuman-i Āthār va Mafākhir-i Farhangī.

Brac de la Perrière, Éloïse (2008), *L'Art du livre dans l'Inde des sultanats*, Paris: Presses de l'Université Paris-Sorbonne.

Brand, Michael and Glenn D. Lowry (1985), *Akbar's India: Art from the Mughal City of Victory*, New York: Asia Society Galleries.

Brend, Barbara and Charles Melville (2010), *Epic of the Persian Kings: The Art of Ferdowsi's Shahnameh*, Cambridge: Fitzwilliam Museum.

Coomaraswamy, Ananda K. (1930), *Catalogue of the Indian Collections in the Museum of Fine Arts, Boston*, 6 vols., Boston: Museum of Fine Arts.

Das, Asok Kumar (2005), *Paintings of the Razmnama, The Book of War*, Ahmedabad: Mapin.

de Blois, François (1992), *Persian Literature*, C. A. Storey (ed.), V/1, London: Royal Asiatic Society.

Digby, Simon (1979), "A Shāh-nāma Illustrated in a Popular Mughal Style," in: Stuart Simmonds and Simon Digby (eds.), *The Royal Asiatic Society: Its History and Treasures*, London: The Royal Asiatic Society, 111-115.

Jahāngīr (1980), *Jahāngīrnāma, Tūzuk-i Jahāngīrī*, Muhammad Hāshim (ed.), Tehran: Bunyād-i Farhang-i Īrān.

Khan, Pasha M. (2012), "Marvellous Histories: Reading the Shāhnāmah in India," *Indian Economic and Social History Review* 49/4, 527–556.

Koch, Ebba (2001), *Mughal Art and Imperial Ideology: Collected Essays*, New Delhi: Oxford University Press.

Lafont, Jean-Marie and Barbara Schmitz (2002), "The Painter Imam Bakhsh of Lahore," in: Barbara Schmitz (ed.), *After the Great Mughals: Painting in Delhi and the Regional Courts in the 18th and 19th Centuries*, Mumbai: Marg, 74-99.

Leach, Linda York (1986), *The Cleveland Museum of Art Catalogue of Oriental Art*, Cleveland: Cleveland Museum of Art.

—— (1995), *Mughal and Other Indian Paintings from the Chester Beatty Library*, London: Scorpion Cavendish.

—— (1998), *Paintings from India, The Nasser D. Khalili Collection of Islamic Art*, v. 8, London: Nour Foundation.

Lentz, Thomas W. and Glenn D. Lowry (1989), *Timur and the Princely Vision: Persian Art and Culture in the Fifteenth Century*, Los Angeles: LACMA.

Leoni, Francesca, *The Revenge of Ahriman: Images of Dīvs in the* Shāhnāma, *ca. 1300-1600*, Unpublished dissertation, Princeton University, 2008.

Losty, Jeremiah P. (1982), *The Art of the Book in India*, London: British Library.

Marshall, D. M. (1985), *Mughals in India: A Bibliographical Survey of Manuscripts*, London: Mansell.

Melville, Charles (2006), "Introduction," *Shahnama Studies I*, Cambridge: The Centre of Middle Eastern and Islamic Studies, University of Cambridge, xix-xxvi.

Parodi, Laura E., et al. (2009), "Tracing the History of a Mughal Album Page in the Los Angeles County Museum of Art," *Asianart.com* (online).

Payeur, Brittany (2009), "The Lilly Shamshir Khani in a Franco-Sikh Context: A Non-Islamic 'Islamic' Manuscript," in: Christiane Gruber (ed.), *The Islamic Manuscript Tradition: Ten Centuries of Book Arts in Indiana University Collections*, Bloomington: Indiana University Press, 221- 248.

Qureshi, Adeela (2012), "Bahram's Feat of Hunting Dexterity as Illustrated in Firdausi's Shahnama, Nizami's *Haft Paikar* and Amir Khusrau's *Hasht Bihisht*," in: Charles Melville and Gabrielle van den Berg (ed.), *Shahnama Studies II: The Reception of Firdausi's Shahnama*, Leiden: Brill, 181-211.

Rizvi, Kishwar (2012), "The Suggestive Portrait of Shah 'Abbas: Prayer and Likeness in a Safavid Shahnama," *Art Bulletin* XCIV, no. 2: 226-250.

Robinson, Basil (1983), *Persian Painting and the National Epic*, London: The British Academy, 275-297.

Schmitz, Barbara (1992), *Islamic Manuscripts in The New York Public Library*, New York: Oxford University Press.

Seyller, John (1999), *Workshop and Patron in Mughal India: The Freer Rāmāyana and Other Illustrated Manuscripts of 'Abd al-Rahīm*, Zurich: Artibus Asiae.

Sharma, Sunil (2003), "Amir Khusraw and the Genre of Historical Narratives in Verse," *Comparative Studies of South Asia, Africa and the Middle East* XXII, no. 1: 112-118.

Simpson, Marianna Shreve (2012), "Šāh-nāma, IV. Illustrations," *EIr* online edition, http://www.iranicaonline.org/articles/sah-nama-iv-illustrations. Accessed 15 May, 2012.

Skelton, Robert W. (1976), "Indian Painting of the Mughal Period," in: Basil Robinson (ed.), *Islamic Painting and the Arts of the Book*, London: Faber and Faber, 233-274.

Sotheby's, Messrs. (1967), *Catalogue of Highly Important Oriental Manuscripts and Miniatures, the Property of the Kevorkian Foundation, 6 December 1967*, London: Sotheby's.

Stanley, Tim (2004), "The Kevorkian-Kraus-Khalili Shahnama. The History, Codicology and Illustrations of a Sixteenth-century Shirazi Manuscript," in: Robert Hillenbrand (ed.), *Shahnama: The Visual Language of the Persian* Book of Kings, London: Ashgate, 85-98.

Swietochowski, Marie Lukens (1994), "The Metropolitan Museum of Art's Small Shāhnāma," in: Marie Lukens Swietochowwski and Stefano Carboni (ed.), *Illustrated Poetry and Epic Images: Persian Painting of the 1330s and 1340s*, New York: Metropolitan Museum of Art, 67-81.

Tavakkul Beg (1999), *Tārīkh-i dilgushā, Shāhnāma-yi nasr*, ed. Ihyā Muhammad Āqāzāda, Tehran: Hawza-yi Hunarī.

Verma, Som Prakash (2002), "Persian and Mughal Painting: The Fundamental Relationship," in: Irfan Habib (ed.), *A Shared Heritage: The Growth of Civilizations in India and Iran*, New Delhi: Tulika, 150-176.

Welch, Stuart Cary (2004), "Zal in the Simurgh's Nest: A Painting by Mir Sayyid 'Ali for a Shahnama Illustrated for Emperor Humayun," in: R. Crill, S. Stronge, and A. Topsfield (ed.), *Arts of Mughal India: Studies in Honour of Robert Skelton*, London: Victoria and Albert Museum, 36-41.

Index

Abaqa 75
'Abd al-Qādir Badā'ūnī 89
'Abd al-Qādir Baghdādī 66
'Abd al-Rahīm Khān-i khānān 94
Abū al-Fazl 90
Abū Ḥanīfa Dīnawārī 65
Abū Manṣūr 'Abd-al-Razzāq 5
Abū Manṣūr Tha'ālibī 65
Afrāsiyāb 14–23, 37, 59, 62, 66–67, 78
Ahrīman 18
Akavān 98
Akbar 89–91, 94, 101, 103, 105
Akbari *Shāhnāma* 90, 101
Akhlāq-i Nāsirī 90
Akvān-dīv 15, 20–21
al-Akhbār al-ṭiwāl 65
'Ālamgīr 87, 89
Amīr Khusraw 86, 90, 95
Anpu 29, 31
Anūshīrvān 5
Anvarī 86, 90
ʿAsjadi 7
'Awfī 99
Awhadī 46, 90
Āzāda 47, 82
Āzād Sarv 8
Āzar Bīgdelī 35

Bābur 87
Badā'ūnī 89–91, 98–99, 105
Bahrām 47, 62–65, 67–68, 77–78, 82, 101
Bahrām Gūr 81–82, 101
Bal'amī 65–66, 70, 101
Bata 29–31
Bayram Khān 98
Bāysonghori Preface v, 1–10
Bāysonghori Recension 3, 7–8, 10
bazm 37
Bīzhan ix, 13–15, 63–65, 67, 78–80, 82
Bīzhan-o Manīzha 13, 15, 16, 19, 20–22, 25
al-Bundarī 61, 68, 70

Dāneshvar the Deqān 3, 5
dāstān 12–16, 19–20, 22–25, 36, 78
Dāstān-i Bīzhan-o Manīzha 13
Dāstān-i Davāzdah Rokh 16
Dāstān-i Furūd-i Siyāvush 25, 59
Dāstān-ī Sohrāb 17, 22, 25

Esfandiyār 17, 23–25
Euripides' *Hippolytus* 28

Farīburz 58–59, 67
Farīdūn/Feridun 23, 24, 36, 37, 40, 75, 81–82, 95
farr 20, 80
Farrokhī 7, 48
Feridun *see* Farīdūn
fitna 42, 47
Furūd 15, 23, 58–69, 72, 76–79, 81–82

Garsivaz 20, 37, 59
Ghazālī 90
Ghurar akhbār mulūk al-Furs 65
Gīv 14–18, 38–39, 58, 62–64, 67–68
Golestān *Shāhnāma* 2
Gorgīn 14–15, 17, 21, 23
Goshtāsp 23
Great Mongol *Shāhnāma* 29
Gūdarz 15, 38–39, 58, 61, 64, 67, 68

Gulistān 90
Gutman *Shāhnāma* 87

Hadīqa 90
Hāfiz 44, 45, 48, 86
haft khwān 23
Haft khwān-i Esfandiyār 24, 25
Haft khwān-i Rostam 25
Hāmāvarān 21, 23, 24, 40
Ḥamd-Allāh Mustawfī 66
Hamzanāma 91
Hātifī 95
Heliodorus' *Æthiopica* 39
Humāyūn 90, 103

Ibn al-Balkhī 66
Ibrahim Sultan *Shāhnāma* 29–30
Ikhtiyārāt-i Shāhnāma 99

Jahāngīr 89, 94–95, 100
Jāmī 29–30, 33, 35, 46–47, 50, 54, 86, 90
jām-i gītī namā 78–79
Jarīra 15, 58–59, 61, 63–64, 68
javāb 32
Javāmi' al-hikāyāt 99

Kalāt 64, 76, 77
Kalīla and Dimna 31
Kay Kāvūs 15, 20–21, 23–24, 36–37, 40, 42, 58, 76, 81
Kay Khusraw 14–18, 20, 24, 42, 47, 58–62, 64–67, 76–82
Kayomarth/Kayūmars 4, 101
Kay Qobād 24, 36
Kayūmars *see* Kayomarth
Khāqānī 44, 90
Khor Firuz 5–7
Khwarazm 31
Kīmiyā-yi Sa'ādat 90

Lughat-i Shāhnāma 66

Mahābhārata 2, 91, 95, 100
Mahmudnāma 48
Manīzha 13–25, 31, 40, 78, 79, 82
mansūkh 50
Manṭeq al-Tayr 46
Manzarī Samarqandī 98
Maqāmāt 76
Mas'ūd Sa'd Salmān 99
Mathnavī-i ma'navī 90
mawbad/mōbad 4, 18
Māzandarān 19–20
Mīr Sayyid 'Alī 103
mōbad see mawbad
Muhammad Jūkī 87
Muhammad Jūkī *Shāhnāma* 89
Mujmal al-tawarīkh 66
Mullā Taqī of Shus[h]tar 99

Naqīb Khān 91
nāsikh 50
Nasirean Ethics 29
Nizāmī 32, 44, 47, 48, 86, 89, 90

Omar 3, 4
'Onṣorī 6–8, 31, 48
oral poetics 1
oral poetry 61
oral tradition 2, 4, 5

Papyrus D'Orbiney 29
Persephone 31
Phaedra 28
Pīrān 14, 15, 17, 19, 37, 58
popular Mughal art 87

Qābūsnāma 90
Qor'an/Qur'an 28, 29, 31, 46, 47, 50
al-Qoshayrī 33

Rāgamālā 95
Rakhsh 19, 103
Rāmāyana 91, 95, 100
razm 37, 61
Rīv 67-68
Rīvnīz 61, 62, 64, 68

Rostam/Rustam 8, 15–25, 37, 39, 42, 43, 59, 66, 78–80, 93, 97, 98, 103
Rūdāba 23, 40, 75, 101, 102
Rudakī 31, 48–50
Rūmī 44, 47, 48, 90
Rustam *see* Rostam

Sa'dī 34, 44, 45, 90
Sām 8, 90
Sanā'ī 44, 90
sarāyanda 61, 63
Shādbahr and 'Ayn al-Hayyāt 31
Shāh 'Ālam II 99
Shahanshāhnāma 98
Shāh Jahān 87–89, 98, 100
Sharaf Manerī 90
Shīrīn 19, 42, 47
Shiʿite 3, 9, 10
Simorgh/*sīmurgh* 4, 103
Sindbad 31
Sindbadnāma 31
Siyar-al-moluk 7
Siyāvosh/Siyāvush 15, 17–19, 22, 25, 28, 30, 31, 36–37, 39–42, 44, 48–52, 58–59, 61, 64–67, 76–77, 81
Sohrāb 17, 23, 25, 37
Sudāba 28, 30, 36, 39–44, 50–52
Sufi 29, 33, 44, 48
Sulṭān Maḥmūd 5, 6, 8, 32, 48

Ṭabarī 33, 42, 65–66, 71, 101
Tahmīna 23
Takht-i Solaymān 75–76, 81–82
Ṭālibī 58, 61, 63, 67
Tārīkh-i dilgushā-yi Shamshīrkhānī 67, 99
Tavakkul Beg 67–68, 99
Thousand and One Nights 31
Timurnāma 95
Transoxania/Transoxiana 39, 50
Tukhvār 61–63, 65–68
Tūrān 14–19, 58–59, 66, 76, 78
Ṭūs 5, 39, 58–62. 64–68, 76–78
Ṭūsī 29, 90

Vakhshī 44
Vāmiq and 'Azrā 31
Vīs 31, 42, 50
Vīs and Rāmīn 42, 50

White Dīv 24
White Idol and Red Idol 31

Xenophon's *Ephesiaca* 30

Yazdgerd 3–5
Yusof ix, 28, 30–35, 42, 44–50, 56
Yusof and Zolaykhā ix, 32, 33, 35, 44, 46–48, 50

Zafarnāmah-yi Shāhjahānī 98
Zahhāk 36, 40, 75, 81–82, 95
Zāl 4, 23, 90, 101–103
Zarāsp 64, 68
Zolaykhā ix, 28–30, 32–35, 44, 46–50, 52